Best Easy Bike Rides
San Francisco

Help Us Keep This Guide Up to Date

Every effort has been made by the author and editors to make this guide as accurate and useful as possible. However, many things can change after a guide is published—trails are rerouted, regulations change, techniques evolve, facilities come under new management, etc.

We appreciate hearing from you concerning your experiences with this guide and how you feel it could be improved and kept up to date. While we may not be able to respond to all comments and suggestions, we'll take them to heart and we'll also make certain to share them with the author. Please send your comments and suggestions to the following address:

Globe Pequot
Reader Response/Editorial Department
246 Goose Lane, Suite 200
Guilford, CT 06437

Or you may e-mail us at: editorial@falcon.com

Thanks for your input, and happy cycling!

Best Easy Bike Rides Series

Best Easy Bike Rides
San Francisco

Wayne D. Cottrell

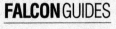

FALCONGUIDES

GUILFORD, CONNECTICUT

FALCONGUIDES®

An imprint of The Rowman & Littlefield Publishing Group, Inc.
4501 Forbes Blvd., Ste. 200
Lanham, MD 20706
www.rowman.com
Falcon and FalconGuides are registered trademarks and Make
Adventure Your Story is a trademark of The Rowman & Littlefield
Publishing Group, Inc.

Distributed by NATIONAL BOOK NETWORK

British Library Cataloguing-in-Publication Information Available

Library of Congress Control Number: 2020950076

ISBN 978-1-4930-5243-1 (paperback)
ISBN 978-1-4930-5244-8 (e-book)

*To my son Tyler, and to the memory of
my mother Barbara and my grandmother Louella*

Contents

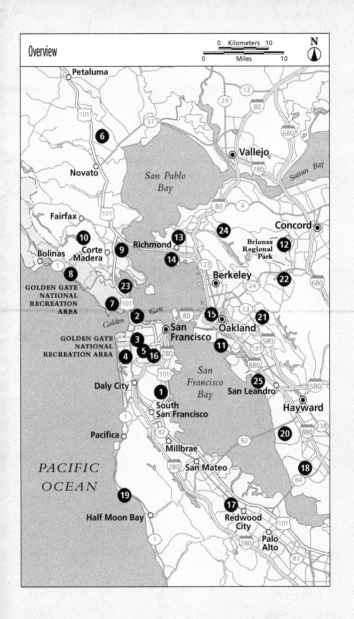

Overview

Kilometers
0   10

Miles
0   10

N

Petaluma

Vallejo

San Pablo
Bay

Suisun Bay

Novato

6

Fairfax

Concord

10   Corte
          Madera

Richmond   24   Briones
                          Regional
                          Park   12

Bolinas

8   9   13   Berkeley   22

GOLDEN GATE
NATIONAL
RECREATION
AREA   23   14

7   2   15   Oakland   21

San
Francisco   11

GOLDEN GATE
NATIONAL
RECREATION
AREA   3

4   5   16

Daly City   25   San Leandro

1   San
          Francisco
          Bay   Hayward

South
San Francisco   20

Pacifica

Millbrae   18

PACIFIC
OCEAN   San Mateo

19   17   Redwood
                    City

Half Moon Bay   Palo
                     Alto

Abstract

This book offers fifteen easy rides, plus ten suggested (also easy) rides, of various lengths and terrain to cover a wide range of abilities. The rides are generally short in length, in keeping with the book's easy theme. None of the rides has long or steep climbs. It is nearly impossible to encounter entirely flat routes in the Bay Area, except along the San Francisco Bay. Even the Pacific Coast is rugged, steep, and often inaccessible. Thus, many of the rides feature a few short climbs and descents. The book is designed for entry-level and beginner cyclists and riders who are not prepared for or do not have the time for a long route. Yet, fit cyclists can find some fun and training in doing any of these rides fast, or maybe two or more times in succession.

The geographical definition of the Bay Area varies according to US Census designations. The San Francisco–San Mateo–Redwood City metropolitan division includes San Francisco and San Mateo Counties (estimated 2018 population: 1,652,900). San Francisco City and County are contiguous, and San Mateo County is often referred to as "the Peninsula." The San Francisco–Oakland–Berkeley metropolitan statistical area (MSA) is the well-known five-county Bay Area and includes Alameda, Contra Costa, Marin, San Francisco, and San Mateo Counties (estimated 2018 population: 4,729,500). The San Francisco Bay Area encompasses an equally well-known nine-county region, adding Napa, Santa Clara, Solano, and Sonoma Counties to the MSA. Finally, the San Jose–San Francisco–Oakland combined statistical area is a massive fourteen-county region, adding Merced,

San Benito, San Joaquin, Santa Cruz, and Stanislaus Counties to the nine-county region (estimated 2018 population: 9,666,100). This book treats San Francisco as the center, emanating from there to incorporate rides in the city, and in Alameda, Contra Costa, Marin, and San Mateo Counties—most of the five-county region.

Introduction

San Francisco Bay is, perhaps, the most well-known and significant geographical feature in California. The Bay covers anywhere from 400 to 1,600 square miles, depending on the inclusion of marshes, tidelands, estuaries, and smaller bays. The Bay's length is up to 60 miles, and its width is up to 12 miles. About 40 percent of California's water drains through the Bay, making it essential to ecosystems and human life throughout the state. The Bay is connected to the Pacific Ocean through the Golden Gate, which was spanned in 1937 by the Golden Gate Bridge. There are a few islands in the Bay, two of which are regularly inhabited (Alameda and Treasure). Alcatraz is a former federal penitentiary, and Angel formerly housed immigrants, particularly the Chinese, who wrote poetry on the walls. Otherwise, habitation is concentrated in urbanized settlements that encircle the Bay, the most populous of which are the cities of Oakland, San Francisco, and San Jose. Four bridges span the Bay—Bay (I-80), Dumbarton (CA 84), Richmond–San Rafael (I-580), and San Mateo (CA 92)—while three others cross Suisun Bay, to the north, which is where the Sacramento and San Joaquin Rivers merge before flowing into San Francisco Bay. Transportation across the Bay includes the aforementioned bridges, which carry cars, trucks, and buses; Bay Area Rapid Transit trains travel across the Bay underwater, in the Transbay Tube. Extensive ferry service across the Bay was reestablished after the 1989 Loma Prieta earthquake damaged and closed the Bay Bridge for a while. The Bay's bridges only recently have been accommodating bicycles; previously, arrangements had to be made with the State Department of Transportation (Caltrans) for a bike shuttle van. Today, only the San Mateo Bridge has no provisions for bicycles; it is now possible to bicycle halfway, but not yet all the way, across the Bay Bridge. The improved accommodations for bicycles exemplify an overall improved climate for bicycling in the Bay Area. Market Street in San Francisco, which is the spine of the city's financial district, has been converted into a transit-bicycle-pedestrian corridor, effectively removing private motor vehicles from the traffic stream. Further, elevated freeway structures in San Francisco, including the Embarcadero Freeway (formerly I-480), and an extended segment of US 101, have been demolished, thereby opening up sightlines, removing depressing shadows, and channeling motor vehicles elsewhere. The notions of replacing a freeway lane with a bike lane and substituting a critical mass of bicycles for a motor vehicles are quite real in San Francisco. The favorable cycling conditions translate into some excellent riding opportunities in San Francisco and around the Bay!

About San Francisco

San Francisco (SF) had an estimated population of 883,300 in 2018, making it California's fourth-largest city. It was California's first major city, and its largest until the mid-1910s, when Los Angeles (LA) overtook it. For the preceding seventy years, and perhaps even today, SF was the gateway to the West Coast of the United States. Thousands flocked to SF in the late 1840s, after gold was discovered in the Sierra Nevada. The city grew rapidly; the population increased from 1,000 to 150,000 in just twenty years. While the population of the LA region is now two to five times that of the SF region, depending on how the regions are defined, SF initially had the best communication, transportation, and water supply in California. The transcontinental railroad first came to SF, and San Franciscans knew about California statehood two months before Los Angelenos learned the news. Even today, LA remains dependent on water from Northern California. Population growth in SF slowed after 1890, in part because of limited space. The city's area is just 46 square miles, and some of that land is fill, over the Bay. Also, the 1906 SF earthquake was very destructive and a huge setback, requiring extensive rebuilding. The population of SF reached 775,357 in 1950 and subsequently decreased over the next thirty years. A comeback and revival of sorts began in the 1980s; today the city has a growing population that is at its highest ever.

San Francisco is recognized as a center of technology, the arts, the sciences, finance, transportation, activism, food, tourism, and general creativity. Its proximity to Silicon Valley, as well as major educational and research institutions (University of California, Berkeley, and Stanford) boost and foster the city's intelligence quotient. Despite the progress, SF has not forgotten about traditional transportation technologies such as the bicycle. The city's nearly 150-year-old cable car system has been upgraded, and it still operates. SF's renowned activism includes the environment, and the bicycle is very much a part of the demands for efficiency and non-motorization. The reader is encouraged to do the rides in this book and then try those in *Best Bike Rides San Francisco*!

About the Bay Area

The San Francisco Bay Area is often referred to as a five-county region. That area, the San Francisco–Oakland–Berkeley metro, incorporates several urbanized areas (UZAs) and urban clusters (UCs), as defined by the US Census, including San Francisco–Oakland, Antioch, Concord, and Half Moon Bay. The San Fransisco–Oakland UZA nonetheless includes some or all of each of the five counties. This book covers the San Francisco–Oakland UZA and the Half Moon Bay UC, equivalent to the metro area minus the Concord and Antioch UZAs. The population of the book's coverage area was 3.92 million in 2010. The region is an economic force, rating as the highest in the world, according to the OECD (Organization for Economic Cooperation & Development), for GDP (gross domestic product) per capita, and labor productivity. Combined with San Jose to the south, the entire region has a one-trillion-dollar economy, putting it on par with all but the world's sixteen largest nations. In terms of recreational opportunities, the Bay Area is rich. The Golden Gate National Recreation Area (GGNRA) is a large (82,027-acre) urban park that stretches from Marin County in the north to San Mateo County in the south. The GGNRA's area of coverage is more than twice the size of SF. Marin County has thirty-four open-space preserves, each with a trails system. The East Bay Regional Parks District is the largest in the United States, managing seventy-three parks and 1,250 miles of trails. The Bay Trail and Bay Area Ridge Trail, both discussed later, offer additional opportunities for recreation and exploration. Other parks and park like entities exist, including the Mount Tamalpais Watershed, East Bay Municipal Utilities District (trail use requires a permit), numerous city parks, state beaches and parks, nearby Point Reyes National Seashore, and bike paths in multiple cities. The Bay Area geography is profoundly affected by the San Francisco Bay and the San Andreas and Hayward Faults. Uplifts from the latter two have created ridges and ranges that generally run northwest-southeast. There are also numerous isolated hills, the most prominent of which is Mount Diablo in the East Bay. Only within a buffer around the Bay is the landscape truly flat. Yet there is enough gentle terrain for a casual cyclist to enjoy, with more opportunities for riding than can fit into one book.

About This Book

The twenty-five rides described in this book include nine in the San Francisco and Peninsula subregion, eleven in the East Bay, and six in Marin County. The terrain in Marin County is the most challenging, hence the fewer number of rides there. There is a map and Miles and Directions section for fifteen of the rides and a text description for the other ten. Each ride's text includes the route (roads and trails), road and trail conditions, traffic information, scenery, history, folklore, special events, culture, and flora and fauna along the way so that riders know what to expect. The descriptions give each route character. To keep riders in the present, the descriptions also discuss demographics, urban issues, and transport infra-structure. A few photographs from the rides should entice readers to get out there and see for themselves. To orient the user, the GPS coordinates of each start-finish point are included. Information on climb lengths and gradients is included as well.

Resources

Bicycling clubs and organizations are abundant in the Bay Area. The main organizations are the Bicycle Trails Council of the East Bay (bicycletrailscouncil.org), Bike Walk Alameda (www.bikewalkalameda.org), Bike East Bay (bikeeastbay.org), Marin County Bicycle Coalition (marinbike.org), Metro-politan Transportation Commission (mtc.ca.gov), Mountain Biking Marin (mountainbikingmarin.com), San Francisco

Bicycle Coalition (sfbike.org), San Francisco Urban Riders (sfurbanriders.org), Silicon Valley Bicycle Coalition (bike siliconvalley.org), Treasure Island Development Authority (sftreasureisland.org), city and county planning and/or engineering departments (particularly those of Alameda, Berkeley, Brisbane, El Cerrito, Fremont, Hayward, Lafayette, Larkspur, Martinez, Mill Valley, Newark, Novato, Oakland, Orinda, Piedmont, Richmond, San Francisco, San Leandro, San Pablo, San Rafael, Sausalito, South San Francisco, and Union City), and the California Department of Transportation (Caltrans; dot.ca.gov). There also are many clubs and teams; at least one of these is bound to fit your needs.

Safety and Equipment

For most of the road routes contained in this book, traffic ranges from minimal to medium-heavy, depending on the time of day you are riding and the day of the week. To be safe, it is paramount to be predictable. If motorists have a good sense of what to expect from you, you'll be safer on the road. Riding with traffic, signaling turns, and generally obeying the same rules that apply to motor traffic are great habits. For the novice, riding with traffic can be easy, especially if there is an adequate shoulder on the road. Riding is even easier when there is a bike lane, and it's easiest when there is a separate bike path.

The door zone—the area where car doors swing open—should be avoided, even if that requires riding farther into the traffic lane. Similarly, you have the right to take the lane when avoiding potholes or other obstacles on the roadside, and you always have the right-of-way along a "sharrow" (shared traffic lane). Cyclists are advised to use special caution at intersections, where drivers make left and right turns. One approach is to assume that drivers do not see you, even when a traffic control gives you the right-of-way.

Busy bicycle paths, such as portions of the Bay Trail, can have a mixture of users, including pedestrians, slow and fast cyclists, recumbent riders, rollerbladers, step-gliders, and others. Some paths separate cyclists from other users, but do not depend on adherence to this. Be alert to all users, and treat paths as shared facilities. If you are a beginning cyclist, then a bike safety class can be useful. People who participate in a good class consistently express how much safer and more comfortable they feel riding in a variety of traffic conditions. Cycling courses also cover other topics, such as bike selection and fit, basics of bike handling, and maintenance.

What should you bring on your ride? Always pack a pump and spare tube or patch kit. A small multi-tool will help with adjustments and minor repairs. Bring lights for front and back—some cyclists use these at all times, including daylight. Bring water, something to snack on, and one more layer than you think you'll need, particularly in cooler weather. With a cell phone and some cash or a card, you are ready to go!

How to Use This Guide

When choosing rides in this book, observe the length, the net elevation difference, the total amount of climbing, and the range of ride times. Road rides range from 2.75 to 18.95 miles. Mountain bike rides range from 2.7 to 8.25 miles. All of the rides in the book have a high-low elevation differential of less than 575 feet. Much of the Bay Area is hilly, though, so these rides are the exception rather than the rule, in terms of their lack of longer climbs. The Ride Finder section lists the distribution of ride distances and elevation changes. The easiest rides, and the best ones to do with children, use bike paths, have less than 100 feet of climbing, and are short in mileage. Note that rides can be improvised by turning around early or by doing two laps of a route rather than one. One way to measure a ride's difficulty is to divide the elevation differential by the distance. The higher the value, the more challenging the ride.

UTM coordinates: Readers who use either a handheld or car-mounted GPS unit can punch in the UTM coordinates for each starting point, and have the GPS lead the way. Use the UTM coordinates with NAD 27 datum (rather than WGS83 or WGS84).

Mileage markers on the map: The distances provided in this book may not match up with distances provided by existing trail maps or your own bike odometer. If you are using a bike odometer, then note these must be calibrated carefully; changing to a larger tire can make a noticeable difference. While GPS devices are generally accurate, they too can be off. Use the mileage data in this book as a rough guide that provides you with a close—but not exact—determination of distance traveled.

Traffic volumes: For the roads ridden in this book, a recent twenty-four-hour, two-way traffic volume is provided. Traffic volumes vary by hour of the day, day of the week, location, and season, so an average is representative of the given road segment. A daily traffic volume of under 5,000 is light; 5,000 to 15,000 is medium; 15,000 to 25,000 is medium heavy; and 25,000 and over is heavy. Some routes use heavily trafficked roads out of necessity, for the scenery, or for the experience.

Times: To assist cyclists with ride planning, a range of estimated times (fast and leisurely) is provided for each ride. My time for the route is also provided and can be used as a benchmark. Note that my times include all stops at traffic signals and stop signs.

Highway, Street, Path, and Trail Names

Highway and street names are taken from street maps and signs. State highways are abbreviated CA. Paths and trails along the Bay Trail are well marked, as are those along the Bay Area Ridge Trail. Other paths are not always marked, or even named. Trails within parks are typically marked with a post at a trailhead or junction. There are plenty of unnamed trails, though, including some that have names but no visible markers. The mileage logs and text descriptions attempt to convey the proper directions to keep you on course.

Road Surface, Shoulder, Path, and Trail Conditions

The road and path surfaces in these rides are, in general, in good condition, unless otherwise noted. Shoulders and shoulder widths are adequate unless otherwise noted. Trail conditions can vary according to the season, level of usage, rainfall and drainage, and maintenance. Some of the trails in the regional parks, and those used by equestrians, can have moguls and exposed and/or loose rocks. Erosion can occur over time, creating fissures. Note that park trails are closed for three days following a rainstorm. Trails also may be closed because of brush fires, construction, or maintenance work.

How to Use the Maps

Each ride map illustrates the given route and starting-ending point against a backdrop of important roads, geographical features, communities, and landmarks. The maps include a limited amount of information, by intention, to emphasize the given route. Selected mile markers, along with the recommended direction of travel, are included on each map. For out-and-back segments, the mile markers generally pertain to the outbound direction of travel. The total length of the ride is listed near the starting-ending point. The scales of the maps vary. If you need more detailed map and location information, please refer to the "map" entry in each ride's header section.

Map Legend

	Transportation		**Symbols**	
≡≡380≡≡	Interstate/Divided Highway	✪	Capital
≡≡101≡≡	US Highway	•—•	Gate
━━1━━	Featured State, or Local Road	17.1◆—	Mileage Marker
——1——	State Highway	🅿	Parking
————	Local Road	▲	Peak
▪▪▪▪▪▪▪▪▪	Featured Bike Route	🎪	Picnic Area
▭▭▭▭▭▭▭	Bike Route	■	Point of Interest
·············	Trail/Dirt Road	○	Town
	Municipal		**❶**	Trailhead (Start)
– – – – –	State Border	🎓	University/College
— — — —	County Border	❓	Visitor Center
	Hydrology		**Land Use**	
⬭	Lake/Reservoir	▭	National Recreation Area
〜	River		
⬯	Marsh	▭	State or Local Park

Easy Ride Finder

Ride	No.	Miles	Bike	Region	Elev. Differential
Around Alameda	11	10.9	road	East Bay	16 ft.
Bahia Ridge to Rush Creek	6	6.9	mtn	Marin	238 ft.
Bair Island to Bayfront	17	8.15	road	SF-Peninsula	11 ft.
Barry Cronkhite Peace Ride	7	8.0	mtn	Marin	569 ft.
Bay Trail San Bruno	1	16.5	road	SF-Peninsula	45 ft.
Bolinas Lagoon Open Loop	8	13.8	road	Marin	54 ft.
Briones: Bovine to Equine	12	4.1	mtn	East Bay	362 ft.
Coyote Hills Untamed	18	6.8	mtn	East Bay	53 ft.
Crossing the Golden Gate	2	7.65	road	SF-Peninsula	266 ft.
Cycling the Coastal Trail	19	11.75	road	SF-Peninsula	45 ft.
Eden Landing Interpretation	20	4.5	mtn	East Bay	8 ft.

Ride	No.	Distance	Type	Region	Elevation
Escape from San Quentin	9	10.6	road	Marin	210 ft.
Garbage Mountain Bayside Mush	13	6.0	mtn	East Bay	8 ft.
Get to the Point Richmond	14	5.9	road	East Bay	33 ft.
Golden Gate Park Outback	3	8.25	mtn	SF-Peninsula	276 ft.
Joaquin Miller Time	21	3.1	mtn	East Bay	155 ft.
Lafayette Reservoir Roleur	22	2.75	road	East Bay	58 ft.
Lap Lake Lagunitas	10	6.35	mtn	Marin	150 ft.
Pickleweed Inlet Open Loop	23	14.05	road	Marin	145 ft.
Sobrante Sojourn	24	3.7	mtn	East Bay	496 ft.
A Spin Through Glen Canyon	16	2.1	mtn	SF-Peninsula	314 ft.
Spokin' Shades of San Leandro	25	13.85	road	East Bay	33 ft.
Sunset to Sherwood via Stern	4	6.4	road	SF-Peninsula	389 ft.
Treasure (Island) Hunt	15	16.4	road	East Bay	224 ft
You See SF: Mount Sutro Trails	5	2.7	mtn	SF-Peninsula	541 ft.

Best Easy San Francisco and Peninsula Rides

San Francisco and San Mateo County, to the south, form the San Francisco–San Mateo–Redwood City metropolitan division. The Peninsula cities of Atherton, Belmont, Brisbane, Burlingame, Colma, Daly City, East Palo Alto, Foster City, Half Moon Bay, Hillsborough, Menlo Park, Millbrae, Pacifica, Redwood City, San Carlos, San Mateo, South San Francisco, Woodside, and a number of unincorporated communities (e.g., El Granada, Emerald Lake, Montara, Moss Beach, Princeton-by-the-Sea) are distinguished from other Bay Area cities by their direct access to San Francisco (i.e., no need to cross a bridge). It was from Sweeney Ridge, in the mountains northeast of Half Moon Bay, that Gaspar de Portolá sighted San Francisco Bay in 1769. The Santa Cruz Mountains run north-south through San Mateo County, effectively splitting the county into western and eastern sides. Urbanization is concentrated on the east side; development is less extensive in the west. The mountains remain mostly undeveloped, with a large portion devoted to the San Francisco State Fish & Game Refuge. Airplanes land at and take off from San Francisco International Airport—which is in San Mateo County—on a constant basis, making the airport the seventh-busiest in the United States. To the south, on the east side, are Santa Clara County and Silicon Valley. To the southwest is Santa Cruz County. At the hub, to the north, is San Francisco (SF). Six of the book's rides are in SF—a seventh ride enters SF from Alameda County; San Mateo County rides are in Brisbane and South San Francisco, the Half Moon Bay area, and Redwood City. The concentration of rides in SF is in line with the book's title. But SF is a great cycling city. Despite the city's hills, there is an extensive network of bike routes and accommodations for bikes. Cycling guides instruct riders on how to avoid the steepest hills. The well-known Critical Mass movement, now nationwide, started in SF. And the city's bike messengers are some of the fastest and most daring around.

1   Bay Trail San Bruno

Start: Brisbane Lagoon Fisherman's Park, Sierra Point Parkway, Brisbane
Length: 16.5 miles (18.95-mile option) (out-and-back route)
Riding time: 1 to 2½ hours (my time:1H19:32 long option; 1H06:21 shorter option)
Terrain and surface: 87 percent paved or concrete paths, 13 percent paved roads
Elevations: Low—4 feet on Bay Trail, north side of Oyster Point

Marina; high—41 feet on Bay Trail south of Point San Bruno Park
Daily traffic volumes: In 2005, estimated 7,400 on Sierra Point Parkway near Marina Boulevard; 3,000 on Marina north of Sierra Point
Map: *The Thomas Guide by Rand McNally—Street Guide: San Francisco County* (any recent year), page 688

Getting there: *By car*: From San Francisco, head south on US 101. Exit at Sierra Point Parkway and keep straight. Look for Brisbane Lagoon Fisherman's Park parking on the right. *By public transit*: Ride Caltrain from central SF to Bayshore Station. Bicycle south on Tunnel Avenue, left on Lagoon Road, and right on Sierra Point Parkway to Brisbane Lagoon Fisherman's Park. Train headways: 10 to 20 minutes during weekday rush hours; hourly on weekdays nonrush; and 90 minutes on weekends. Starting point coordinates: 37.686517°N / 122.390653°W

The Ride

Bay Trail San Bruno is a 16.5-mile out-and-back road bike ride, with an 18.95-mile option. The length is at the limits of "easy," but it is about as flat a ride as one can find in the Bay Area, with an elevation change of just 45 feet. Despite the name, the ride never enters the city of San Bruno; it starts in

SAN FRANCISCO BAY TRAIL

San Francisco Bay was "discovered" in 1769 by Spanish explorer Gaspar de Portolá when he looked out from atop Sweeney Ridge, on the San Mateo Peninsula. Records show that a European ship pilot named de Morena probably saw the Bay in 1579, when, after recovering from sickness after being dropped off to the north, walked past the bay on his way to Mexico. Yet, long before these explorers came, the Ohlone lived along the bay for thousands of years, until 10,000 B.C., when they had to evacuate because of rising waters. Fast-forward to today, and the bay is recovering from the modern-day effects of dredging, dumping, and filling. More reclamation and recovery are needed, but segments of the bay that were formerly muddy, trashy, or used for industrial purposes are now accessible. The San Francisco Bay Trail project has the ambitious goal of completely encircling the Bay with a bike-pedestrian path and/or trail. The completed Bay Trail will be 500 miles long; just over 70 percent of it was complete as of this writing. We cannot wait for the other 30 percent!

Brisbane and continues into South San Francisco. San Bruno Point is along the way, though, while San Bruno Mountain, to the northwest, overlooks the route. Start at Brisbane Lagoon Fisherman's Park in Brisbane, heading south on Sierra Point Parkway. After passing under US 101, turn left on Marina Boulevard. After .25 mile, make a U-turn adjacent to Ultragenyx Pharmaceutical, followed by a right turn onto Bay Trail. From here, the ride hugs the San Francisco Bay along the Bay Trail, making a series of 90-degree bends, and crossing a few bridges to remain waterside. Development along the trail mostly consists of the back sides of industrial buildings, plus a hotel. San Francisco Bay is in full view. The trail passes a series of marinas and parks, including Brisbane/

Sierra Point Marina, Oyster Cove Marina, Oyster Point Marina, Oyster Point Park, and San Bruno Point Park. After 8.3 miles, the route reaches Airport Boulevard, just north of San Francisco International Airport. This is a turnaround point. An optional longer route continues along the walkway adjacent to Airport Boulevard, turning left onto the path (Bay Trail) adjacent to North Access Road. The midpoint of this option is a loop of the "SamTrans" bulb, which is a near-island containing a San Mateo Transit bus yard. The path around the bulb was rough and bumpy when I rode this in July 2020. Unlike the main route, the optional extension crosses a few driveways and a signalized intersection. Riders who want to avoid the motor vehicle action, the extra miles, and the bumpy bulb path can turn around at Airport Boulevard. Return via the reverse of the outbound route.

Miles and Directions

0.0 Start at Brisbane Lagoon Fisherman's Park; head south on Sierra Point Parkway.

0.8 Pass under US 101.

1.0 Traffic signal at Marina Boulevard; turn left (note: damaged pavement on Marina).

1.2 U-turn through median opening adjacent to Ultragenyx Pharmaceutical.

1.25 Right onto Bay Trail (paved path).

1.35 Take a 90-degree bend right; trail is now bayside.

1.6 Take a 90-degree bend right; Brisbane/Sierra Point Marina at left.

2.0 Take 90-degree bends right and left (mile 2.35).

2.55 Follow sweeping curve right.

2.8 Take 90-degree bend left; cross bridge.

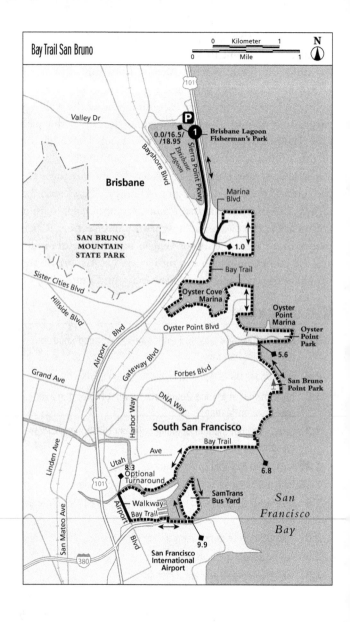

Bay Trail San Bruno

0   Kilometer   1

0   Mile   1

N

Valley Dr

P

1 Brisbane Lagoon
Fisherman's Park

0.0/16.5/
/18.95

Bayshore Blvd

Brisbane Lagoon

Sierra Point Pkwy

Brisbane

Marina
Blvd

1.0

SAN BRUNO
MOUNTAIN
STATE PARK

Bay Trail

Sister Cities Blvd

Hillside Blvd

Oyster Cove
Marina

Oyster
Point
Marina

Oyster
Point
Park

Airport   Blvd

Oyster Point Blvd

5.6

San Bruno
Point Park

Gateway Blvd

Forbes Blvd

Grand Ave

DNA Way

Harbor Way

South San Francisco

6.8

Linden Ave

Bay Trail

Ave

8.3
Optional
Turnaround

SamTrans
Bus Yard

San
Francisco
Bay

Utah

101

Walkway
Bay Trail

9.9

San Mateo Ave

Airport   Blvd

San Francisco
International
Airport

380

3.15 Take 90-degree bend left.

3.2 Follow 90-degree bend left.

3.8 Curve left; Oyster Cove Marina at left.

4.0 Take right-hand 90-degree bend (and at miles 4.3 and 4.5).

4.65 Bear left at fork.

4.7 Left to remain on Bay Trail—enter Oyster Point Park; Oyster Point Marina at left.

5.25 Take 90-degree bend right.

5.3 Bear left at fork.

5.6 Follow 90-degree bend left; cross bridge.

5.75 Bear left at fork.

6.15 Take 90-degree bend left; enter San Bruno Point Park.

6.2 Take 90-degree bends left and right (miles 6.4 and 6.6).

6.65 Turn left; cross bridge.

6.7 Take 90-degree bends left and right (mile 6.8).

7.4 Curve left.

8.0 Turn left; cross bridge.

8.05 Follow 90-degree bend right.

8.3 Arrive at Airport Boulevard; turn around here (optional route continues).

Return route; turns, parks, and marinas included; details on bends and curves excluded:

8.6 Right at end of bridge.

9.95 Right at end of bridge; enter San Bruno Point Park.

11.35 Enter Oyster Point Park; Oyster Point Marina at right.

11.9 Right after leaving Oyster Point Park.

12.6 Pass Oyster Cove Marina at right.

14.6 Pass Brisbane/Sierra Point Marina at right.

15.35 End of Bay Trail; right on Marina Boulevard.

15.5 Traffic signal at Sierra Point Parkway; turn right.

15.7 Pass under US 101.

16.5 End ride at Brisbane Lagoon Fisherman's Park.

Optional route from mile 8.3:

8.3 Left onto walkway adjacent to Airport Boulevard; cross series of driveways.

8.4 Traffic signal at Belle Air Road; keep straight.

8.5 Left onto path adjacent to North Access Road.

8.7 Bear left to remain on Bay Trail.

8.85 Take 90-degree bend right; cross bridge.

8.9 Left at end of bridge.

9.1 Take 90-degree bend left; begin "SamTrans bulb" loop (note: bulb path is rough and bumpy)

9.5 Curve right; horn of bulb (stay left at fork on far side of bulb).

9.9 End of bulb loop; take a right on Bay Trail, cross bus yard entrance; begin return ride (reverse outbound route).

Bike Shop

Ocean Cyclery, 1935 Ocean Ave., San Francisco, (415) 239-5004, oceancyclery.com.

2 Crossing the Golden Gate

Start: Fort Point National Historic Site, end of Marine Drive, San Francisco

Length: 7.65 miles ("skinny" counterclockwise loop, with clockwise loop at northern end, and short out-and-back segment)

Riding time: 30 to 80 minutes (my time: 38:44)

Terrain and surface: 65 percent concrete and paved paths, 28 percent paved roads, 7 percent limited-access road

Elevations: Low—6 feet on Moore Road at Horseshoe Bay; high—272 feet on path adjacent to off-ramp to Alexander Avenue

Traffic and hazards: 72 percent of the route is on car-free paths; heavy car and bus parking activity on north side of bridge is possible.

Map: *The Thomas Guide by Rand McNally—Street Guide: San Francisco County* (any recent year), page 647

Getting there: *By car:* From central San Francisco (SF), follow US 101 through town via Van Ness Avenue, Lombard Street, Richardson Avenue, and Doyle Drive; exit at Lincoln Boulevard (last SF exit). Take a left on Lincoln, a left on Long Avenue, and stay left on Marine Drive; continue to the parking area at Fort Point. Note that parking areas near the bridge were being closed intermittently during the COVID-19 pandemic. *By public transit:* San Francisco Municipal Transportation Agency (MUNI) bus route 28 runs between the Sunset District and North Point, near Fisherman's Wharf, with a stop at Fort Point. Route 28 runs every 10 minutes on weekdays, every 20 minutes on weekends. Starting point coordinates: 37.810358°N / 122.476772°W

The Ride

Crossing the Golden Gate Bridge may be on nearly everyone's bucket list, so why not cross on a bicycle? It is a short (7.65 miles) and mostly slow—because of foot traffic on the bay side—but memorable trip. Because of the bridge's popularity, and to prevent complete chaos, bicycles and pedestrians have some regulations. The bridge has two sides: east (northbound for vehicles) and west (southbound for vehicles). Pedestrians are permitted only on the east (bay) side. Cyclists may use either side. Dogs (except service dogs), powered scooters, rollerblades, and skateboards are all prohib-

GOLDEN GATE BRIDGE

The Golden Gate Bridge was completed in 1937, after four years of construction. The bridge is 4,200 feet in length, less than a mile, but was the longest single-span structure in the world at the time of its construction. The record was finally surpassed in 1964 by New York City's Verrazano-Narrows Bridge, which itself has since been surpassed by fifteen others. Even though it no longer holds the record, the American Society of Civil Engineers still lists the Golden Gate Bridge as one of its Seven Wonders of the Modern World. Joseph Strauss designed the bridge as early as 1917, although co-designers Leon Moisseiff and Irving Morrow later contributed heavily to the final project. Special notice goes to Charles Alton Ellis, who, for a while, worked up to seventy hours a week on the engineering for no pay, producing volumes of calculations. Today, the bridge carries about 112,000 motor vehicles daily, and a large number of pedestrians and bicyclists. Regarding the latter, 200,000 non-motorists crossed the bridge on opening day. Motorists must pay a toll ranging from $5 (carpools) to $8 when entering SF; there is no northbound toll. On the dark side, eleven workers were killed during the construction of the bridge (including ten in one day), and the bridge remains the world's second-most-used by suicide jumpers. Positive notes are that nineteen workers who fell from the bridge were saved by safety netting. Also, construction continues on a safety system for suicide jumpers, although the project had been delayed as of this writing.

ited. From March to November, the bridge's east side is open to pedestrians from 5 a.m. to 9 p.m. On weekdays, cyclists may ride from 5 a.m. to 3:30 p.m., and then from 6:30 p.m. to 5 a.m., after gaining security clearance. (Clearance involves being spotted on a camera; a gate is then opened automatically). On weekends, the cycling hours are 5 a.m. to 9 p.m. From November to March, the hours are similar, except that weekend security clearance hours start at 6:30 p.m. The bridge's west (ocean) side is open to cyclists only from November to March on weekdays from 5 a.m. to 3:30 p.m., and weekends from 5 a.m. to 9 p.m. Security clearance hours are from 9 p.m. to 5 a.m. daily. From March to November, the cycling hours are 5 a.m. to 3:30 p.m. on weekdays, and 5 a.m. to 6:30 p.m. on weekends. Security clearance hours are 6:30 p.m. to 5 a.m. daily. Note that there are some hours during which no bicycles are allowed. When I rode this in July 2020, the west side was closed for unexplained reasons; all cyclists had to use the east side. Riding on the east side is typically slow because of the presence of pedestrians. Riding on the west side is slowed by bridge towers that have narrow passages. On either side it is best to relax and enjoy the ride! Most of the route is on both the Bay and Bay Area Ridge Trails. After the ride, a visit to the Fort Point National Historic Site should also be on your bucket list.

Miles and Directions

0.0 Start from the parking area at Fort Point National Historic Site; head east on Marine Drive.

0.3 Bear right on Long Drive (climb: 5.7% grade).

0.5 Turn right on Battery East Trail (paved path—heavily used).

0.95 Sharp left onto Coastal Trail (paved path).

1.0 Trail curves 180 degrees right.

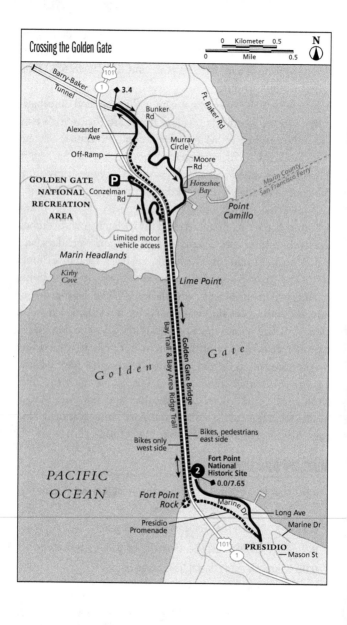

Crossing the Golden Gate

Barry-Baker Tunnel

◆ 3.4

Bunker Rd

Alexander Ave

Murray Circle

Off-Ramp

Moore Rd

GOLDEN GATE
NATIONAL
RECREATION
AREA

Conzelman Rd

Horseshoe Bay

Marin County /
San Francisco Ferry

Point Camillo

Limited motor
vehicle access

Marin Headlands

Kirby Cove

Lime Point

Golden Gate

Bay Trail & Bay Area Ridge Trail

Golden Gate Bridge

PACIFIC OCEAN

Bikes, pedestrians
east side

Bikes only
west side

❷

Fort Point
National
Historic Site

0.0/7.65

Fort Point Rock

Marine Dr

Long Ave

Marine Dr

Presidio Promenade

101
1

PRESIDIO

Mason St

0   Kilometer   0.5
0   Mile   0.5

N

1.05 Right onto the Golden Gate Bridge walkway (east side).

1.25 Trail is now over water.

2.3 Bridge is over Lime Point (Marin County).

2.6 Conzelman Road is below.

2.75 Pathway veers right, away from US 101.

2.8 Cross paved area accessing parking lot; bear left to ride parallel to US 101.

3.1 Pathway veers away from US 101; right on Alexander Avenue.

3.25 Left on West Bunker Road.

3.4 Right, in advance of tunnel, then right again, to continue on West Bunker Road.

3.5 Pass under Alexander Avenue.

3.95 Stop sign at Murray Circle; turn right.

4.05 Stay right at Center Road; now on Moore Road.

4.1 Horseshoe Bay is at left.

4.25 Stay right at fork; now on Conzelman Road (Bay Trail; limited vehicular access).

4.35 Pass under US 101; begin climb (switchbacks—8.7% grade).

4.8 Leave Bay Trail segment; right into parking area.

4.85 Veer right onto path to Golden Gate Bridge (west side).

5.0 Conzelman Road is below.

5.35 Now the trail is over water.

6.35 Now the trail is over land (Fort Point).

6.6 Leave bridgeway; right onto Coastal Trail; trail loops right and passes under US 101.

6.65 Stay left at fork—continue on Battery East Trail.

7.1 Leave path; turn left on Long Drive (descent).

7.35 Stop sign at Marine Drive; turn left.

7.65 End ride at Fort Point National Historic Site.

Bike Shops (San Francisco)

Golden Gate Bridge Bike Rentals, 2157 Lombard St., (628) 444-3385, goldengatebridgebikerentals.com

Roaring Mouse Cycles, 934 Mason St., (415) 753-6272, roaringmousecycles.com

Trek Bicycle San Francisco Cow Hollow, 3001 Steiner St., (415) 346-2242, https://www.trekbikes.com/retail/san_francisco_cow_hollow/

3   Golden Gate Park Outback

Start: John F. Kennedy Drive & Hagiwara Tea Garden Drive, Golden Gate Park, San Francisco.
Length: 8.25 miles (lollipop plus figure eight), with shorter 1.45 and 6.8 mile options.
Riding time: 40 to 90 minutes (my time: 1H13:31, on foot)
Terrain and surface: 52 percent gravel and dirt trails, 23 percent paved paths, 25 percent paved park roads.
Elevations: Low—16 feet at south end of Park and Ocean Railroad Trail; high—292 feet on Phil Arnold Trail.
Traffic and hazards: On Sundays, 100 percent of the ride is car-free, except for six street crossings. On Saturdays in 2016, JFK Drive carried 12,000 vehicles per day near Conservatory Drive East.
Map: *The Thomas Guide by Rand McNally—Street Guide: San Francisco County* (any recent year), page 667

Getting there: *By car*: From central SF, head westward on I-80 to US 101 freeway north, to end of freeway. Keep straight via Octavia Boulevard, left on Fell Street to Golden Gate Park entrance. Keep straight via John F. Kennedy (JFK) Drive. Left on Kezar Drive, right on Martin Luther King (MLK) Drive, right to continue on MLK, right on Music Concourse Drive to Music Concourse Parking Garage entry. *By public transit*: MUNI bus route 44 travels between the Richmond District and Hunter's Point, passing through Golden Gate Park via the Music Concourse. Headways are 10 to 20 minutes daily. MUNI bus routes 5, 7, 18, 21 & 33 all serve the park's bordering streets; MUNI light-rail line N from central SF stops one to two blocks from the park's south border. Starting point coordinates: 37.772575°N / 122.466672°W

The Ride

Golden Gate Park is a mecca for San Francisco's urban outdoor enthusiasts, including cyclists. Given that it is the third-most-visited park in the United States, expect to share the roads, trails, and paths with other users, especially on weekends. Sundays are particularly busy with non-motorists, as John F. Kennedy Drive, the park's main east-west road, is closed to motor vehicles. Golden Gate Park is not known for its trail riding. Despite the park being over 140 years old, the Golden Gate Park Multi-Use Trail Program was underway as of this writing, with the objective of officially designating trails in the park. There are currently enough trail segments to patch together a fun, mostly off-road ride, though. The full Golden Gate Park Outback ride is 8.25 miles, with a shorter western option of 6.8 miles, and a really short eastern option of 1.45 miles. The Miles and Directions section describes the routing. The park generally slopes upward from west to east, although there are rolling hills in between. San Francisco Urban Riders have mapped the lengths and profiles of the park's trails (although their elevation differentials seem to be exaggerated). The park is a busy but peaceful place, it is dense with meadows, wooded areas, small lakes, memorials, and attractions. The following are passed along the way: Robert Burns statue (Scottish poet; composer of "Auld Lang Syne"), John McLaren Rhododendron Dell (Scottish horticulturalist; superintendent of Golden Gate Park for fifty-three years), Phil Arnold Trail (open space advocate who worked for the city for thirty-three years), McLaren Lodge, Oak Woodlands (several wooded areas), Conservatory of Flowers (greenhouse and botanical garden that is on the National Register of

GOLDEN GATE PARK

Golden Gate Park covers 1,017 acres in western San Francisco, in a 5-mile-long by 0.5-mile-wide rectangle, and a 0.7-mile-long, block-wide "panhandle." At the heart of the park's design is the work of John McLaren (1846–1943), who was superintendent for fifty-three years, well into his eighties. McLaren was friends with naturalist John Muir and knew the park designs of Frederick Law Olmsted, including that of New York's Central Park. McLaren put his familiarity to good use in planting tens of thousands of trees in Golden Gate Park (he would plant two million trees in various places in his lifetime). He also integrated numerous meadows and open spaces into the park design, with plenty of natural buffers. As for the latter, McLaren dedicated some forty years to building up a natural berm on the west side of the park to keep sand from drifting into the park. The Murphy and Dutch Windmills on the western edge of the park were designed to pump water into the park, thereby having both aesthetic and practical functions. McLaren detested statues and might have wanted to obscure the park's memorials behind shrubbery; otherwise, John McLaren and Golden Gate Park are a nearly inseparable pair.

Historic Places), Redwood Grove, Lloyd Lake, Mallard Lake, Bernice Rodgers Way Trail (named for a city resident, who was 101 years old as of this writing), South Lake and Middle Lake, Chain of Lakes Meadow, Speedway Meadow, Polo Fields (contains a three-quarter-mile paved cycling track), East Meadow, Prayerbook Cross, Strawberry Hill (waterfall, pedal boats), Doughboy Meadow, Pioneer East Meadow, Mothers' Grove, Rose Garden, and the World War I Memorial. As for road names, Makoto Hagiwara managed the park's Japanese Tea Garden for thirty years. And we all know JFK and MLK!

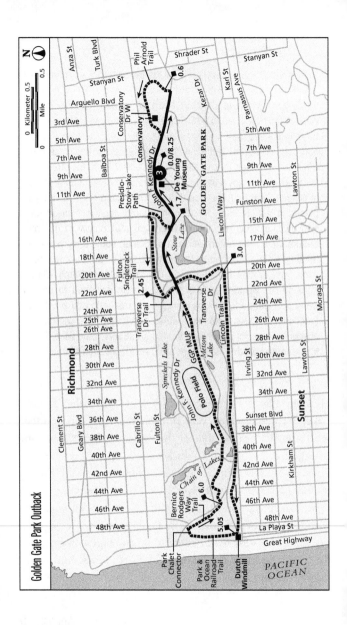

Golden Gate Park Outback

Miles and Directions

0.0 Start at John F. Kennedy Drive and Hagiwara Tea Garden Drive in Golden Gate Park, just north of the Museum Concourse; head east on JFK Drive.

0.55 Left on Conservatory Drive East.

0.6 Immediate right on Phil Arnold Trail (dirt); trail climbs to the ride's highest elevation (292 feet).

1.0 End of trail; keep straight across Arguello Boulevard and continue along Conservatory Drive West (descent).

1.2 Right on JFK Drive. (Note: You can end the ride at Hagiwara Tea Garden Drive, at the 1.45-mile mark; or you can start the ride here and head west.)

1.7 Right on Presidio–Stow Lake path (paved).

1.95 End of path at Fulton Street; cross Park Presidio Drive (signal) and continue onto Fulton Singletrack Trail (wider than single-track).

2.45 Cross Crossover Drive and Transverse Drive in succession.

2.5 End of trail; left on Transverse Drive Path North (gravel).

2.6 End of path; cross JFK Drive, bear left, then right on Transverse Drive Singletrack Trail.

2.95 End of trail at Transverse Drive; cross Transverse, then cross Martin Luther King Drive; keep straight on path.

3.0 Right on the paved path.

3.05 Left on Lincoln Trail (mixture of double- and single-track, and some sand).

5.05 End of trail; cross MLK Drive and continue onto Park and Ocean Railroad Trail (gravel; lowest elevation of ride: 16 feet).

5.55 Right on Park Chalet Connector (paved path; no marker).

5.65 Right on Bernice Rodgers Way Trail—use road or parallel paved path.

6.0 End of Bernice Rodgers Way; turn left onto Golden Gate Park Multi-Use Path (GGP MUP; paved) near road's junction with MLK Drive.

6.15 Bear right, then right again to continue on GGP MUP.

6.25 Cross Chain of Lakes Drive East.

6.6 Stay left at fork.

6.65 Polo Fields at left (bicycle racing track on perimeter).

6.85 Stay right at fork.

7.35 GGP MUP is now parallel to JFK Drive.

7.45 Cross Transverse Drive and continue on JFK Drive (i.e., ride in road).

7.5 Pass under Crossover Drive.

8.25 End ride at Hagiwara Tea Garden Drive.

Bike Shops (San Francisco)

Bay City Bike Rentals and Tours, 622 Shrader St., (415) 346-2453, baycitybike.com.

Everybody Bikes, 1352 Irving St., (415) 682-4439, everybodybikessf.com.

Freewheel Bike Shop, 1920 Hayes St., (415) 752-9195, thefreewheel.com.

San Francyclo, 746 Arguello Blvd., (415) 831-8031, sanfrancyclo.com.

4 Sunset to Sherwood via Stern

Start: Vale Avenue Parking Lot, Stern Grove Dog Park, 100 Vale Ave., San Francisco

Length: 6.4 miles (clockwise loop)

Riding time: 25 to 75 minutes (my time: 35:22)

Terrain and surface: 80 percent paved roads, 20 percent paved paths

Elevations: Low—15 feet, on Vicente Street at Lower Great Highway; high—404 feet at Ulloa Avenue and Kensington Way

Traffic and hazards: Portola Drive carried 18,800 daily vehicles west of Laguna Honda Boulevard in 2019; CA 35 (Sloat Boulevard) carried 30,000 vehicles west of CA 1 in 2017; Ulloa Avenue carried 1,500 daily vehicles east of Kensington Way in 2017; and Wawona Street carried 1,000 daily vehicles west of 34th Avenue in 2016.

Map: *The Thomas Guide by Rand McNally—Street Guide: San Francisco County* (any recent year), page 667

Getting there: *By car*: From central San Francisco, head south on US 101. Exit at Ocean Avenue; turn right. Turn right on 19th Avenue (CA 1), then left on Sloat Boulevard (CA 35). Turn right on Crestlake Avenue, then right on Vale Avenue; enter Stern Grove and park in Vale Avenue lot. *By public transit*: MUNI bus route 23 travels between Hunter's Point and the Sunset District, passing Stern Grove on its south side via Sloat Boulevard. MUNI bus route 28 travels between Fort Point and Daly City BART, passing Stern Grove on its east side via 19th Avenue. MUNI light-rail line L travels between central San Francisco and the Sunset District, stopping on Taraval Avenue three blocks north of Stern Grove. Starting point coordinates: 37.736633°N / 122.482558°W

The Ride

San Francisco is home to a host of communities that are worth exploring. Not all of them are suitable for easy cycling, though, given the city's renowned hills. Sunset to Sherwood via Stern is a 6.4-mile road ride that cruises through the comparatively flat neighborhoods on SF's southwest side, passing through the Sunset District, West Portal, and Miraloma Park, and then climbing to skim the edges of Sherwood Forest, St. Francis Wood, Stonestown, and Merced Manor. The Sunset is San Francisco's largest community, with a population of about 85,000. The Sunset is also SF's foggiest, particularly the Outer Sunset (west of Sunset Boulevard), because of its proximity to Ocean Beach. You may encounter fog on this journey, as only the late summer and early autumn months are fog-free. On the far corner of the Outer Sunset, on Sloat Boulevard, the ride passes the San Francisco Zoo and the Dalia Fleishhacker Memorial Building (on the National Register of Historic Places) on the left. The ride also passes through Pine Lake Park and Sigmund Stern Grove via paved paths. Sigmund Stern was a philanthropist and a nephew of jeans magnate Levi Strauss. Stern Grove has been the site of an annual series of concerts and festivals since 1932. There is some climbing and descending on the eastern part of the ride, but the route turns before reaching the bigger hills to the east. There are either bike lanes or sharrows on Portola Avenue, Sloat Boulevard west of 22nd Avenue, and Vicente Street. Just under half of the route is on the Bay Area Ridge Trail (BART; see sidebar).

BAY AREA RIDGE TRAIL

Not to be confused with the Bay Trail, the Bay Area Ridge Trail (BART—not to be confused with Bay Area Rapid Transit) is yet another ambitious non-motorization project. Similar to its counterpart the Bay Trail, the BART plan is to encircle the Bay Area via a series of paths, trails and appropriate roads. Unlike the Bay Trail, which borders the Bay, the BART concept is to connect interior parks and open spaces, using ridges as needed, to form a fully connected outer circle around the Bay. The ultimate length will be 550 miles—10 percent longer than the Bay Trail's 500. Two-thirds of it had been completed as of 2015. (A completed segment may not involve new construction). The BART is not as jagged as the Bay Trail, enabling it to extend as far north as Calistoga (Napa County), and as far south as Gilroy (Santa Clara County), and still be only 10 percent longer. The trail's official starting point is the Golden Gate Bridge. This ride uses a portion of the end of the loop—you are permitted to pretend as if you have done the entire BART when passing impressed bystanders. The project began in 1987, and was the idea of William Penn Mott, Jr., who was the director of the National Park Service at the time (he had previously worked for the East Bay Regional Parks District). Two hikers completed the loop in 1999, despite the project being unfinished.

Miles and Directions

0.0 Start at the Vale Avenue parking lot in Stern Grove, adjacent to the dog park; head west on a paved path.

0.05 Right on the connector path.

0.1 End of connector; turn right on unnamed path.

0.3 End of path at parking lot; cross parking lot, then resume path.

0.35 End of path; turn right on Stern Grove Entry Road (begin switchbacks—6.3% grade).

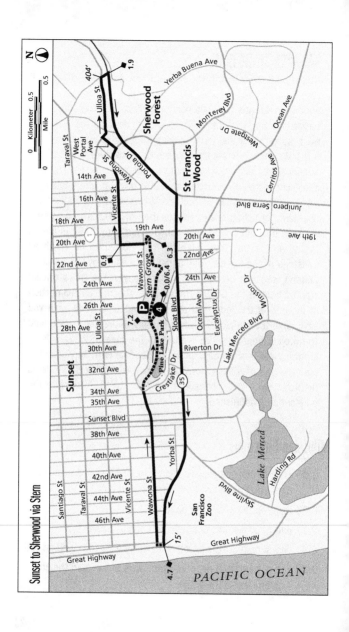

Sunset to Sherwood via Stern

0.75 End of path and switchbacks; continue across Wawona Street and onto 20th Avenue.

0.9 Stop sign at Vicente Street; turn right—steady climb (5.0% grade).

0.95 Traffic signal at 19th Avenue (CA 1); keep straight.

1.0 Stop sign at 18th Avenue, and at 17th Avenue (mile 1.05), 16th Avenue (mile 1.15), 15th Avenue (mile 1.2), 14th Avenue (mile 1.25), and Madrone Avenue/Wawona Street (mile 1.35); keep straight on Vicente at each intersection (gradient eases east of 14th Avenue).

1.4 Traffic signal at West Portal Avenue; turn left, cross the railroad track.

1.5 Right on Ulloa Street.

1.55 Stop sign at Claremont Boulevard and at Dorchester Way (mile 1.7); climb at 5.0% grade east of Claremont.

1.85 Stop sign at Kensington Way; turn right.

1.9 Traffic signal at Portola Avenue; turn right.

2.25 Traffic signals at Claremont Boulevard, Vicente Street (mile 2.35), and 14th Avenue (mile 2.5); keep straight on Portola at each intersection.

2.75 Traffic signal at West Portal Avenue (5-way intersection); take easy right onto Sloat Boulevard; cross four railroad tracks (skewed—exercise caution).

2.95 Traffic signal at 19th Avenue (CA 1), and at 34th Avenue (mile 3.85), 45th Avenue (mile 4.5), and 47th Avenue (mile 4.65); keep straight on Sloat Boulevard at each intersection.

4.7 Right on path between (Lower) Great Highway and Upper Great Highway.

4.85 Right on connector path

4.9 Cross (Lower) Great Highway; keep straight onto Vicente Street (lowest elevation of ride: 15 feet).

5.0 Stop sign at 46th Avenue, and at 45th Avenue (mile 5.05), 42nd Avenue (mile 5.25), 41st Avenue (mile 5.3), 40th Avenue (mile 5.35), 39th Avenue (mile 5.4), and 39th Avenue (mile 5.45); keep straight on Vicente at each intersection.

5.55 Right on 37th Avenue.

5.65 Stop sign at Wawona Street; turn left.

5.7 Traffic signal at Sunset Boulevard; keep straight.

5.8 Stop sign at 34th Avenue; keep straight.

5.85 Right on unnamed path; enter Pine Lake Park (chain at entry requires a dismount—beyond chain, path is downhill—7.2% grade)

6.1 Bear left to continue on path (watch for dogs).

6.3 Right on connector path.

6.35 End of connector path; left on path.

6.4 Arrive back at the Vale Avenue Parking Lot.

Bike Shop

Bike Doctor, 2455 27th Ave., San Francisco, (415) 759-7431; repairs

5 You See SF: Mount Sutro Trails

Start: Millberry-Union public parking garage, University of California, San Francisco, 500 Parnassus Ave.
Length: 2.7 miles (counterclock-wise loop, plus out-and-back segment)
Riding time: 20 to 60 minutes (my time: 45:46, on foot)
Terrain and surface: 60 percent dirt trails, 38 percent paved roads, 2 percent stairs

Elevations: Low—365 feet at Parnassus Avenue and Willard Street; high—906 feet atop Mount Sutro.
Daily traffic volumes: 7,480 on Clarendon Avenue in 2016
Map: *The Thomas Guide by Rand McNally—Street Guide: San Francisco County* (any recent year), page 667

Getting there: *By car*: From central San Francisco, head west-ward on I-80 to US 101 North, to end of freeway. Keep straight onto Octavia Boulevard. Turn left on Fell Street. Near Golden Gate Park, exit right, then turn left onto Stanyan Street. Turn right on Parnassus Ave-nue to the parking garage, just past Hillway Avenue. *By public transit*: MUNI light-rail line N travels between central San Francisco and the Sunset District, stopping adjacent to the University of California, San Francisco, campus on Carl Street. MUNI bus routes 6 and 43 travel along Parnassus Avenue, stopping near the UCSF garage. Starting point coordinates: 37.763881°N / 122.457264°W

The Ride

You See SF: Mount Sutro Trails is a hilly but short off-road ride around and over Mount Sutro, just south of the University of California, San Francisco (UCSF) campus. (UCSF is a major research university and medical school, ranked number one in the world in 2019 by *Clinical Medicine*.) At

THE SEVEN HILLS OF SAN FRANCISCO

San Francisco has a lot more than seven hills, but seven are most prominent: Mount Davidson, Mount Sutro, Nob Hill, Rincon Hill, Russian Hill, Telegraph Hill, and Twin Peaks. The tallest is Davidson, at 927 feet, while Sutro and Twin Peaks both top 900 feet. The most densely developed are Nob (also known as "Snob," home to some of SF's finest real estate), Russian (home of Lombard Street, the most crooked in the world), and Telegraph (site of Coit Tower). Each hill has its own story; the city's newspaper—*San Francisco Chronicle*—went so far as to publish a column on each of over 40 hills during the 1950s. Mount Sutro is unique in that 80 percent of it is forested with eucalyptus trees. A portion of the other 20 percent is in Rotary Meadow, which is a garden of native California plants. The Mount Sutro Open Space Reserve and Interior Green Belt overlap, with the former owned by the UCSF, and the latter owned by the city. The mount is named for Adolph Sutro (1830–1898), who made a fortune in the legendary Comstock Lode and then bought ranch property that covered most of the mountain. Sutro's plan to develop residential neighborhoods there never materialized. The massive, 977-foot Sutro Tower (TV and radio antenna), once the tallest structure in SF, is not on Mount Sutro, but on a nearby hill that was formerly named Mount Olympus.

2.7 miles, the ride is short enough to be classified as "easy" and tough enough to give any cyclist a workout. The climbs and descents are short, but steep. The route consists of a "collapsed" clockwise loop, plus an out-and-back segment. The "collapse" in the loop brings the rider to the crest of Mount Sutro. The loop begins on Historic Trail. Part of the "historic" nature is Sutro's former use as a Nike Missile launch site. The ride passes through the UCSF Mount Sutro Open Space Preserve and Interior Green Belt. A staircase near the beginning and end of the ride prevents anyone from not dismounting at least once. It is an enjoyable ride, though, and, in the clearings between the eucalyptus trees, you will definitely "see SF" from Sutro! A short segment of the ride rounds a blind curve on Clarendon Avenue—use the walkway here. Use caution on the descents; the general approach is to sit back on the saddle and to keep the tail end of your bicycle down. The trails are shared with other users. The routing reflects COVID-19 restrictions on bike travel directions as of this writing.

Miles and Directions

0.0 Start from the Millberry Union parking garage; head east on Parnassus Avenue.

0.1 Turn right on Willard Street, followed by a right on Farnsworth stairs (walk bicycle).

0.15 End of staircase; left on Edgewood Avenue (10.1% uphill grade).

0.35 End of paved road; continue onto Edgewood Trail.

0.5 Bear right at junction with Lower Historic Trail and North Ridge Trail; still on Edgewood.

0.55 Cross Medical Center Way (paved road); veer right onto Historic Trail (one-way uphill for bicycles).

0.95 Keep straight at West Ridge Trail junction.

1.15 Historic Trail ends at South Ridge Trail junction—curve left onto Quarry Road (dirt trail).

1.3 Turn right on Clarendon Trail.

1.45 End of Clarendon Trail; turn left onto Clarendon Road walkway (stay on left side of road).

1.55 Turn left on Johnstone Drive (paved road).

1.7 Keep straight at Medical Center Way, then turn right on East Ridge Trail (Mount Sutro climb).

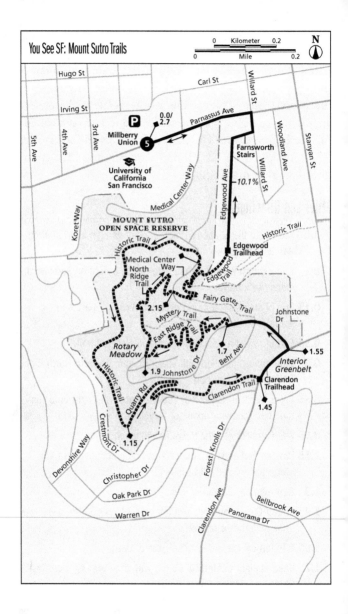

You See SF: Mount Sutro Trails

0   Kilometer   0.2

0   Mile   0.2

N

Hugo St

Carl St

Willard St

Irving St

Parnassus Ave

Woodland Ave

Stanyan St

5th Ave

4th Ave

3rd Ave

0.0/
2.7

P

Millberry
Union

5

Farnsworth
Stairs

Willard St

University of
California
San Francisco

Medical Center Way

Edgewood Ave

10.1%

Koret Way

MOUNT SUTRO
OPEN SPACE RESERVE

Medical Center Way

Historic Trail

Historic Trail

Edgewood
Trailhead

Medical Center
Way

North
Ridge
Trail

Edgewood Trail

Fairy Gates Trail

2.15

Mystery Trail

Johnstone
Dr

East Ridge Trail

Rotary
Meadow

1.7

Behr Ave

1.55

Interior
Greenbelt

1.9   Johnstone Dr

Historic Trail

Quarry Rd

Clarendon Trail

Clarendon
Trailhead

Crestmont Dr

1.45

1.15

Devonshire Way

Christopher Dr

Forest Knolls Dr

Oak Park Dr

Clarendon Ave

Bellbrook Ave

Warren Dr

Panorama Dr

1.75 Keep straight at Mystery Trail; still on East Ridge Trail.

1.9 Crest of Mount Sutro (906 feet); bear right at Rotary Meadow, then right onto North Ridge Trail.

1.95 Keep straight at Mystery Trail; still on North Ridge Trail.

2.15 Cross Medical Center Way; continue descent on North Ridge Trail.

2.2 Keep straight at junction with Lower Historic Trail, continuing onto Edgewood Trail.

2.35 End of trail; keep straight on Edgewood Avenue.

2.55 Take a right on Farnsworth stairs (walk bicycle).

2.6 Take a left on Willard Street, followed by a left on Parnassus Avenue.

2.7 Arrive back at the parking garage.

Bike Shops (San Francisco)

American Cyclery, 510 Frederick St., (415) 664-4545, americancyclery.com

Avenue Cyclery, 756 Stanyan St., (415) 387-3155, avenue cyclery.com

Best Easy Marin County Rides

Marin County is contiguous with the San Rafael metropolitan division, which is one of three divisions that make up the San Francisco–Oakland–Berkeley metro area. Unlike many California counties, Marin County has been able to resist extensive growth. The NIMBY (not-in-my-backyard) sentiment was prevalent in Marin early on, such that a lot of the county has looked the same for decades. Associated with that has been the preservation of open space. An examination of a map of Marin County reveals that there is only one through freeway, there is no BART service, CA 1 still winds and twists its way from the Bay to the coast, and a large area surrounding Mount Tamalpais remains in a natural, undeveloped state. The famous Dipsea running race, from Mill Valley to Stinson Beach, is the oldest trail-running race in the United States, and it sticks to its tradition of age-graded start times. There is legislation that allows the town of Bolinas (see page 45) to be "off the grid" in terms of road signage. Yet, despite the apparent closed society, there is plenty of shared innovation in Marin. Mountain biking was pioneered by Marin County cyclists in the late 1970s, although similar inventions were occurring in Crested Butte, Colorado, around the same time. There are no large cities in Marin—the two largest, Novato and San Rafael, each have populations of less than 60,000. The geographical sphere of influence of Mount Tamalpais, as well as that of the San Andreas Fault—which runs northwest-southeast on the western side of the county—are such that much of Marin's terrain is hilly and often steep. Many bayside areas are hilly, too, making it difficult to find "easy" bicycling in the county. This book describes six relatively easy rides, distributed to Larkspur and San Rafael, Mill Valley and Strawberry, Novato, Stinson Beach and Bolinas, the Marin Headlands, and the Mount Tamalpais Watershed. A seventh ride enters Marin from San Francisco.

6 Bahia Ridge to Rush Creek

Start: Rush Creek Park, Basalt Creek, Novato (park along Bugeia Lane, west of Valley Memorial Park and Cemetery)

Length: 6.9 miles (clockwise loop)

Riding time: 45 to 100 minutes (my time: 1H25:00, on foot)

Terrain and surface: 88 percent fire roads (dirt), 12 percent paved roads

Elevations: Low—3 feet on Pinheiro Fire Road adjacent to Cemetery Marsh; high—241 feet at the crest of Bahia Ridge Fire Road

Traffic and hazards: Traffic volume data unavailable.

Map: *The Thomas Guide by Rand McNally—Street Guide: Marin County* (any recent year), page 526

Getting there: *By car*: From central San Francisco, follow US 101 through town via Van Ness Avenue, Lombard Street, Richardson Avenue, and Doyle Drive to Golden Gate Bridge—continue through Marin County via US 101 freeway. Exit at Atherton Avenue in Novato; turn right. Turn left on Bugeia Lane; Rush Creek Park is at left. *By public transit*: Golden Gate Transit bus routes 54, 54C, 56X, 58, and 70 all serve the Atherton Avenue Bus Pad, at US 101 and Atherton Avenue, 1 mile west of Rush Creek Preserve. The former four lines are commuter buses, running southbound to San Francisco in the morning, and northbound from San Francisco in the evening, on weekdays. Route 70 operates hourly, daily, between San Fransisco and Novato. Starting point coordinates: 38.119197°N / 122.546333°W

The Ride

Bahia Ridge to Rush Creek is a 6.9-mile mountain bike ride through Rush Creek Preserve, in extreme northeast Novato. Although the preserve is 31 miles from central San Francisco, it is easy to access, being just east of US 101, off Atherton Ave-

NOVATO

Technically, Bahia Ridge to Rush Creek is just outside the Novato city limits. Yet, the ride is close enough to Novato to be part of its sphere of influence. Novato had an estimated population of 55,660 in 2018, making it Marin County's second-most-populous city. Novato has been designated as a "best place to live" by livability.com. The city encompasses the sites of three ancient Coast Miwok villages: Chokecherry, Olompali, and Pupuyu. The city's name probably comes from that of a Miwok leader who was called Saint Novatus by Spanish missionaries. Modern-day Novato began to sprout in the mid-nineteenth century: The first school was built in 1859, the railroad came in 1879, and a church and post office were built in the 1890s. The former Hamilton Air Force Base was adjacent to Novato. The base was deactivated in 1974 and was later declared a historic district. It is now being converted into housing and office development. Famous Novatans include astronaut Yvonne Cagle, Super Bowl quarterback Jared Goff, and legendary baseball pitcher Lefty Gomez.

nue. The ride takes advantage of the preserve's mixture of flora and fauna, including wetlands segments, where you may be able to view marshlands, tidal flats, and up to two hundred different species of waterfowl. The route passes the "foreboding" Cemetery Marsh, but have no fear of dead bodies or zombies. There is also a low ridge segment, on the east side of the preserve, where there are groves of manzanita, black oak, and California bay trees. There is some climbing and descending to and from the ridge, plus some uphill and downhill on road.

Miles and Directions

0.0 Start from Rush Creek Preserve trailhead on Bugeia Lane, northeast of Atherton Avenue; head west on Bugeia.

Bahia Ridge to Rush Creek

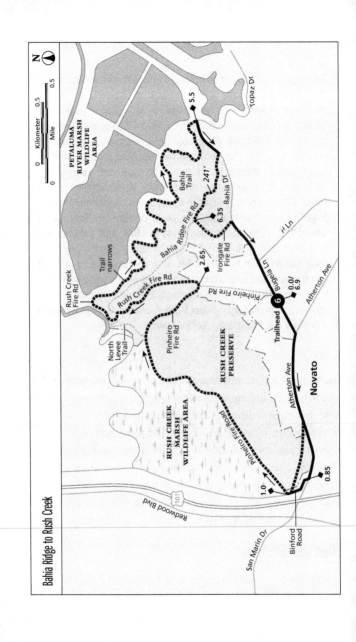

0.15 Right on Atherton Avenue; ride in road or parallel dirt path (use caution at street crossings).

0.85 Right on Binford Road (or use single-track bypass trail, but the descent is tricky).

1.0 Right on Pinheiro Fire Road (dirt); Cemetery Marsh at left.

2.3 Pinheiro Fire Road curves right at North Levee Trail.

2.65 Stay left at junction; now on Rush Creek Fire Road (dirt).

3.2 Easy right at junction (i.e., middle trail); still on Rush Creek Fire Road

3.25 Stay right at junction.

3.35 Trail narrows; now on Bahia Trail.

5.5 End of trail; right on Bahia Drive (climb: 11.1% grade).

5.7 Right on Bahia Ridge Fire Road (climb: 5.4% grade).

6.1 Left on Irongate Fire Road (descent: 12.0% grade).

6.35 End of trail; right on Bahia Drive.

6.6 Stay right at fork; now on Bugeia Lane.

6.9 Arrive back at the Rush Creek Preserve trailhead.

Bike Shops (Novato)

Bicycle Brüstop, 830 Grant Ave., (415) 408-3363, bicycle brustop.com
Class Cycle, 1531 Novato Blvd. #B, (415) 897-3288
Gravy Wheels, 1648 Novato Blvd., (415) 454-9000, gravy wheels.com

7 Barry Cronkhite Peace Ride

Start: Parking area adjacent to Bunker and Simmonds Roads, Marin Headlands, Golden Gate National Recreation Area

Length: 8.0 miles (clockwise loop, separable into 3.7-mile and 4.3-mile loops)

Riding time: 20 to 90 minutes (my times: 38:07 for the shorter loop; 42:58 for the longer loop; 1H21:05 for the entire route, all on foot)

Terrain and surface: 62 percent dirt roads and trails; 38 percent paved roads

Elevations: Low—10 feet at the trailhead at the end of Mltchell Road; high—579 feet at McCullough and Conzelman Roads (Julian Trail trailhead) for the eastern option; 342 feet at Coastal Trail and Old Bunker Road for the western option.

Traffic and hazards: Traffic volume data on Bunker Road unavailable.

Map: *The Thomas Guide by Rand McNally—Street Guide: Marin County* (any recent year), page 626

Getting there: *By car*: From central San Francisco, follow US 101 through town via Van Ness Avenue, Lombard Street, Richardson Avenue, and Doyle Drive to Golden Gate Bridge—continue into Marin County via US 101 freeway. Exit at Alexander Avenue; turn right. Turn left on West Bunker Road; continue through tunnel (one-way; up to a 5-minute wait for a green signal). Continue on Bunker Road to the parking area on the right, adjacent to Simmonds Road. *By public transit*: MUNI bus route 76X operates between central San Francisco and the Marin Headlands (Bunker Road) hourly on weekends only. Starting point coordinates: 37.832714°N / 122.516819°W

The Ride

The Marin Headlands are hilly and rugged, even along the Pacific coastline, making it challenging to find an "easy" ride. Rodeo and Gerbode Valleys represent the Headlands' easiest terrain, although hills are still plentiful. The full Barry Cronkhite Peace Ride is an 8.0-mile mountain bike ride through and up and down the hillsides of these valleys. The 901 feet of climbing in the ride negates its "easy" classification, but the route can be split. The eastern 3.7-mile half, which is more challenging, climbs 499 feet from Rodeo Valley to the Hawk Hill environs; the reward is a majestic view of the Golden Gate Bridge on clear days. The western 4.3-mile half climbs 332 feet to overlook Rodeo Lagoon and Beach and the ocean. Both options pass historical sites. Choose the half that most suits you, or try the entire ride. There is no "Barry Cronkhite"; the title refers to Forts Barry and Cronkhite, two former military installations (see sidebar). The forts have been long deactivated, but there always seems to be a need for a peace ride. Both loops include trail and road segments, in which Bunker Road is the spine. The Julian Trail portion of the eastern loop is part of the Bay Area Ridge Trail. The trail passes near a historic rifle range and Fort Barry. Near the beginning of the western loop, Bunker Road curves along the edge of Rodeo Lagoon. Opposite the lagoon, on its ocean side, is Rodeo Beach, which is known for its unique red and green sand pebbles. The western route also passes the Marin Headlands Visitor Center, Fort Cronkhite, a blue whale skeleton, Hawk Tail Beach, Battery Townsley (see sidebar), Marin Headlands Nursery, and the Marine Mammal Center.

BARRY CRONKHITE

There is no Barry Cronkhite, as the ride title refers to Forts Barry and Cronkhite, two separate assemblies. Fort Cronkhite, named for US Army General Adelbert Cronkhite, was built in the late 1930s. With WWII came a rapid expansion of the fort, and numerous wooden structures were constructed, particularly in 1941. Soldiers stationed there manned artillery, including a large, three-gun antiaircraft weapon. After WWII, the fort was converted to Cold War use and managed the nearby SF-88 Nike Missile launch site. Operation of this continued until the fort closed in 1974. Many of the fort's temporary wooden structures still remain, with the entire fort on the National Register of Historic Places, and can be visited as a Golden Gate National Recreation Area attraction. (Some of the buildings are not open to the public, but there is no military activity.) On a ridge nearby, Battery Townsley—named for WWI Major General Clarence P. Townsley—featured a large magazine and gun installation. The battery was manned at all times during its active years and is now open to the public on the first Sunday of each month. Fort Barry, which is to the south of the ride's Julian Trail segment, predates Fort Cronkhite by over thirty years. Barry, like Cronkhite, was decommissioned in 1974. Fort Barry was steeped in weaponry, with up to seven batteries. The fort also contains a balloon hangar, built in 1921, when the US Army was experimenting with tethered coastal defense balloons. The hangar is one of only two in the United States and is the only one to have actually housed a balloon.

Miles and Directions

0.0 Start at parking area adjacent to Bunker and Simmonds Roads in the Marin Headlands; head east on an unnamed trail.

0.05 Left on Smith Trail.

0.15 End of Smith; right on Rodeo Valley Trail; gradual climb (3.0% grade).

0.85 Right at junction to remain on Rodeo Valley Trail; cross wooden bridge.

0.95 End of trail; right on Bunker Road, followed by an immediate left on McCullough Road; steep climb (8.1% grade).

1.85 Right on Julian Trail (restroom adjacent); begin downhill.

2.5 Keep straight at junction.

3.15 Historic rifle range at right; Fort Barry at left.

3.4 End of trail at Bunker Road; turn left.

3.7 Starting point at right; option to end ride here *or* begin western loop.

4.3 Rodeo Lagoon at left; Bunker Road curves right, then left.

4.6 Stop sign at Mitchell Road; stay left; now on Mitchell Road (Rodeo Lagoon and Beach at left, Fort Cronkhite at right).

5.1 End of road; continue onto Coastal Trail; begin steep climb (9.0% grade).

5.75 Battery Townsley at left.

5.8 Veer right at T junction, onto Old Bunker Road; begin downhill.

6.6 Keep straight; now on Bunker Road (paved); parking at left, Marin Headlands Nursery at right.

6.8 Stop sign at Mitchell Road; turn left; still on Bunker.

7.05 Veer left, across road, onto Miwok Trail.

7.55 Right on Bobcat Trail.

7.65 Sharp right onto Rodeo Valley Trail.

7.9 Right on Smith Trail.

7.95 End of Smith Trail; right on unnamed trail.

8.0 End of western loop and ride; arrive back at the parking area.

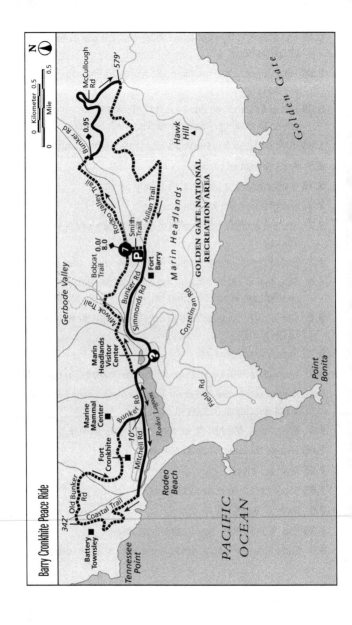

Barry Cronkhite Peace Ride

Bike Shops (Sausalito)

Cleary Bikes, 4000 Bridgeway #310, (415) 528-5437, cleary bikes.com.

Mike's Bikes of Sausalito, 1 Gate 6 Rd., (415) 332-3200, mikesbikes.com.

Sausalito Bike Rentals, 34 Princess St., (415) 331-2453, sausalitobikerentals.com.

8 Bolinas Lagoon Open Loop

Start: Stinson Beach Park, 3514 Shoreline Highway (CA 1), Stinson Beach

Length: 13.8 miles (out-and-back)

Riding time: 40 to 100 minutes (my time: 47:06)

Terrain and surface: 100 percent paved roads

Elevations: Low—8 feet on CA 1 adjacent to Bolinas Lagoon; high—62 feet on Olema-Bolinas Road just north of Bolinas

Traffic and hazards: CA 1 carried 4,800 vehicles daily adjacent to Bolinas Lagoon in 2017.

Map: *The Thomas Guide by Rand McNally—Street Guide: Marin County* (any recent year), page 605

Getting there: *By car:* From central San Francisco, follow US 101 through town via Van Ness Avenue, Lombard Street, Richardson Avenue, and Doyle Drive to Golden Gate Bridge. Continue into Marin County via US 101 freeway. Exit at Shoreline Highway (CA 1). Turn left at Miller Avenue to continue on CA 1. Continue through Golden Gate National Recreation Area to Stinson Beach Park, in Stinson Beach, at left. *By public transit:* Marin Transit bus route 61 travels between Sausalito and Bolinas, via Stinson Beach, four times on weekdays, and ten times on weekend days. To get to Sausalito from San Francisco, ride the Golden Gate Sausalito Ferry from the Ferry Terminal. Starting point coordinates: 37.898011°N / 122.641286°W

The Ride

Bolinas Lagoon is an inlet from the Pacific Ocean. The lagoon is nearly closed at its entry point: The gap between the town of Bolinas on the left and the Seadrift peninsula on the right is only about 120 feet. It is too wide to pedal or jump across, though. Hence, Bolinas Lagoon Open Loop

BOLINAS

Bolinas is just 13 miles as the crow flies from San Francisco, but the town's eclecticism and reclusiveness set it worlds apart. Bolinas is an unincorporated community with a population of 1,620 in 2010. Ground access to Bolinas is indirect, as indicated by the twisting, winding, "getting there" route to Stinson Beach, followed by this ride's route to Bolinas. Locals began to remove signage to their town a while back, deliberately making it difficult to locate. Any questions of the legality of the residents' actions were negated when an official Marin County sign-removal measure was approved during an election. The Bolinas sentiment may have been best captured in a separate measure prepared by local Jane Blethen, also known as Dakar, which refers to clean water, blueberries, bears, skunks, and foxes. She points out the excess of machines and technology, noting that the aforementioned creatures need a place in which to coexist with "the airplanes flying over." The measure was unanimously approved in 2003. The town has resisted new development, even to the extent of limiting new sewerage and capping any expansion of the water supply. Residents on the mesa in the western part of town still travel on dirt roads and use septic systems. Portions of the mesa have eroded into the ocean over time, in part because no preventive infrastructure was ever constructed. Yet, "Bolinans" will not dismiss you—visitors to the Bolinas Museum are welcome, and some creative local artwork is for sale.

is an out-and-back ride between Stinson Beach and Bolinas. The ride starts at Stinson Beach Park and heads toward Bolinas on CA 1. To the right is the Golden Gate National Recreation Area (GGNRA) and Bolinas Ridge. The redwood trees are thick in the forests above—getting up there after the ride is highly recommended. CA 1 hugs the lagoon's east shore, passing by several gulches. At the horn of the lagoon,

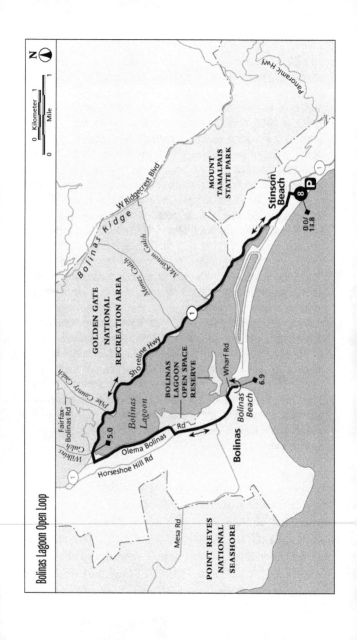

Bolinas Lagoon Open Loop

0.0/13.8

5.0

6.9

8

W Ridgecrest Blvd

Bolinas Ridge

GOLDEN GATE NATIONAL RECREATION AREA

McKinnon Gulch

Morses Gulch

Pike County Gulch

Shoreline Hwy

1

Fairfax-Bolinas Rd

Wilkins Gulch

1

Horseshoe Hill Rd

Olema Bolinas Rd

Bolinas Lagoon

BOLINAS LAGOON OPEN SPACE RESERVE

Wharf Rd

Bolinas Beach

Bolinas

Mesa Rd

POINT REYES NATIONAL SEASHORE

MOUNT TAMALPAIS STATE PARK

Stinson Beach

Panoramic Hwy

P

1

N

0   Kilometer   1
0   Mile   1

the route leaves CA 1 to head south into Bolinas. A segment of Olema-Bolinas Road hugs the west shore. The only short climb in the ride passes through a gap to the north of town (5.8% grade). The ride continues through Bolinas' commercial district to the end of the road at Bolinas Beach before returning.

Miles and Directions

0.0 From the entrance to Stinson Beach Park on CA 1 (Shoreline Highway), head northwest (GGNRA at right).

0.8 Stinson Gulch at right.

1.65 McKinnan Gulch at right.

2.2 Morses Gulch at right.

3.3 Audubon Canyon and Garden Club Canyon at right.

3.7 Pike County Gulch at right.

4.45 Wilkins Gulch at right.

4.5 Left on Fairfax-Bolinas Road.

4.6 Stop sign at Olema Bolinas Road; turn left.

5.75 Stop sign at Horseshoe Hill Road; turn left, still on Olema-Bolinas.

6.6 Enter Bolinas's commercial district as road bends left.

6.7 Road bends right; now on Wharf Road.

6.9 End of road at entrance to Bolinas Beach; turn around here.

7.1 Road curves right; now on Olema Bolinas Road.

7.2 Leave Bolinas's central district.

8.05 Stop sign at Horeshoe Hill Road; turn right, still on Olema Bolinas.

9.2 Right on Fairfax-Bolinas Road.

9.3 Stop sign at CA 1; turn right.

13.8 Arrive back at the entrance to Stinson Beach Park.

Bike Shops (Mill Valley)

Mad Dogs & Englishmen Bike Shop, 129 Miller Ave. #802, Mill Valley Lumber Yard, (415) 326-5141, http://mad dogscarmel.com

Studio Velo, 31 Miller Ave., (415) 380-1882, studiovelo cycling.com

Tam Bikes, 357 Miller Ave., (415) 389-1900, tambikes.com

9 Escape from San Quentin

Start: Remillard Park, East Sir Francis Drake Boulevard, Larkspur
Length: 10.6 miles (counterclockwise loop)
Riding time: 35 to 100 minutes (my time: 49:34)
Terrain and surface: 73 percent paved bike paths, 25 percent paved roads, 2 percent concrete walkways

Elevations: Low—1 foot at Irwin Street and Lincoln Avenue in San Rafael; high—212 feet on "upper" Via La Cumbre, in Larkspur
Traffic and hazards: Traffic volume data unavailable.
Map: *The Thomas Guide by Rand McNally—Street Guide: Marin County* (any recent year), page 586

Getting there: *By car*: From central San Francisco, follow US 101 through town via Van Ness Avenue, Lombard Street, Richardson Avenue, and Doyle Drive to Golden Gate Bridge; continue through Marin County via US 101 freeway. Exit at Sir Francis Drake Boulevard in Larkspur; turn right. Look for Remillard Park on the right, just past the ferry terminal. *By public transit*: From the Golden Gate Ferry Terminal near the foot of Market Street in San Francisco, ride the Larkspur Ferry to Larkspur. Remillard Park is just east of the Larkspur Ferry Terminal. Ferries run daily, at varying frequencies. Starting point coordinates: 37.944075°N / 122.503758°W

The Ride

Escape from San Quentin—well, unless you are a convict—does not stage at the famous prison (see sidebar). Remillard Park is just down the road, on Sir Francis Drake Boulevard. An escaped convict might not follow this route, which is a 10.6-mile road ride through San Rafael and northeastern Larkspur. The ride starts in Larkspur and immediately enters San Rafael, Marin County's most populous city

SAN QUENTIN

San Quentin State Prison is the oldest in California (1852) and has the largest number of males on death row in the Western Hemisphere, with over seven hundred as of this writing. Although women on death row are held in Chowchilla, their executions also occur at San Quentin. Despite the notoriousness of many of the inmates, San Quentin is known for its progressiveness, including the only newspaper published by prisoners, a Vietnam veterans group that gives toys to visiting children, an adult inmate-troubled juvenile program, a drama workshop, a series of baseball games against nonconvicts, and others. Most of the programs are not available to death-row inmates, although the last execution there was in 2006. The land that San Quentin occupies, which borders the San Francisco Bay, has become prime real estate over time. No word on the prison moving, perhaps to make room for the Bay Trail, though. Famous musicians have given concerts here, including B. B. King (1990's *Live at San Quentin*) and 1969's *Johnny Cash at San Quentin*. Both albums won Grammy Awards. As for the latter, in the audience during the concert was an incarcerated Merle Haggard. He said that the performance inspired his own musical career.

(estimated 58,700 in 2018). The hairiest parts of the ride come early, passing San Quentin State Prison, and 0.3 mile on the shoulder of I-580. From there, the route turns for a jaunt along the Bay Trail. Later the ride crosses San Rafael Creek to spin through central San Rafael, which can also be hairy as drivers jockey for position on one-way roads and at stoplines. The ride then heads southeast for some residential road climbing and to enter Larkspur. The US 101 interchange at Sir Francis Drake Boulevard can be avoided by using the adjacent bike paths. East of US 101, to the right, is the Larkspur Ferry Terminal. Farther down, on the left, is the Green Brae Brick Yard, also known as the Remillard Brick Kiln, a prehistoric brickmaking facility on the National Register of Historic Places.

Miles and Directions

0.0 From Remillard Park, head east on Sir Francis Drake Boulevard.

0.75 Keep straight onto I-580 ramp.

1.0 Now on I-580; continue along shoulder.

1.3 Exit I-580.

1.5 Stop sign at Main Street; turn left and pass under I-580.

1.55 Left on East Francisco Boulevard.

2.4 Right on Pelican Way.

2.45 Stop sign at Kerner Boulevard; keep straight.

2.6 Veer left at Glacier Point, onto bike path.

2.75 T junction at Bay Trail; turn left.

2.85 Keep straight at fork.

3.05 Stay right at fork.

3.35 Right at T junction.

4.0 Curve left at junction, followed by a right on Spinnaker Point (paved road).

4.05 Left on unnamed bike path.

4.45 End path; right on Bellam Boulevard.

4.65 Traffic signal at Kerner Boulevard; keep straight.

4.8 Traffic signal at East Francisco Boulevard; turn right.

5.15 Traffic signal at Medway Road; keep straight.

5.8 Road curves right, then turns left; keep straight; now on Grand Avenue.

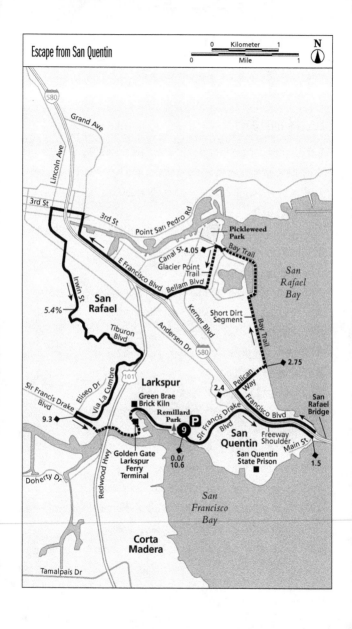

Escape from San Quentin

Kilometer
0 — 1

Mile
0 — 1

N

580

Grand Ave

Lincoln Ave

3rd St

3rd St

Point San Pedro Rd

Pickleweed Park

Canal St 4.05

Bay Trail

E Francisco Blvd

Glacier Point Trail

Irwin St

San Rafael

Bellam Blvd

San Rafael Bay

5.4%

Kerner Blvd

Short Dirt Segment

Tiburon Blvd

Andersen Dr

580

Bay Trail

Sir Francis Drake Blvd

Eliseo Dr

Via La Cumbre

101

Larkspur

Green Brae Brick Kiln

Remillard Park

P

9

Pelican Way

Francisco Blvd

2.75

2.4

9.3

Sir Francis Drake Blvd

San Rafael Bridge

San Quentin

Freeway Shoulder

Main St

Redwood Hwy

Golden Gate Larkspur Ferry Terminal

0.0/ 10.6

San Quentin State Prison

1.5

Doherty Dr

San Francisco Bay

Corta Madera

Tamalpais Dr

5.85 Cross San Rafael Creek.

5.9 Traffic signal at 2nd Street; keep straight.

5.95 Traffic signal at 3rd Street; turn left (3rd Street is one-way).

6.1 Traffic signal at Irwin Street; keep straight and pass under US 101.

6.15 Traffic signals at Hetherton Street and Tamalpais Avenue (mile 6.2); keep straight at each intersection.

6.25 Traffic signal at Lincoln Avenue; turn left.

6.3 Traffic signal at 2nd Street; keep straight.

6.45 Cross San Rafael Creek.

6.6 Traffic signal at Irwin Street; turn right.

6.7 Traffic signals at Andersen Drive and Woodland Avenue (mile 6.9); keep straight at each intersection.

7.2 Begin climb (5.4% grade) at Harte Avenue.

7.85 Right on Tiburon Boulevard.

8.25 Tiburon Boulevard curves right; US 101 at left.

8.35 Tiburon Boulevard curves right at Bret Harte Road; now on Via La Cumbre; enter Larkspur.

8.4 Stay right at fork; "upper" Via La Cumbre climbs briefly at 11.0% grade.

8.85 Stop sign at Via Hermosa; keep straight.

8.9 Stay right at fork short, steep descent.

9.25 Stop sign at Eliseo Drive; turn left.

9.3 Traffic signal at Sir Francis Drake Boulevard; turn left.

9.4 Veer right onto walkway at Del Monte (do not ascend the overpass).

9.5 End of path at T-junction; turn left onto path adjacent to Corte Madera Creek.

9.85 Pass under US 101 freeway structure; cross wooden bridge.

9.95 End of bridge; turn right onto path, adjacent to ferry terminal.

10.1 Traffic signals at Larkspur Landing Circle (two in succession); keep straight.

10.6 Arrive back at Remillard Park.

Bike Shops (Larkspur)

Larkspur Cycle, 556 Magnolia Ave., (415) 891-3376, www .larkspurbike.com

Village Peddler, 1111 Magnolia Ave., (415) 461-3091, www.villagepeddler.com

10 Lap Lake Lagunitas

Start: Lake Lagunitas parking lot, Sky Oaks Road, Mount Tamalpais Watershed (south of Fairfax)
Length: 6.35 miles (bar-bell-shaped route with two clockwise loops)
Riding time: 30 to 75 minutes (my time: 1H05:52, on foot)
Terrain and surface: 52 percent dirt trails, 47 percent paved roads, 1 percent stairs.

Elevations: Low—660 feet on Bullfrog Fire Road at Azalea Trail; high—810 feet on Lagunitas Fire Road, at the lake's southeastern corner.
Traffic and hazards: 100 percent of the ride is on trails and lightly used roads.
Map: *The Thomas Guide by Rand McNally—Street Guide: Marin County* (any recent year), page 585

Getting there: *By car:* From central San Francisco, follow US 101 through town via Van Ness Avenue, Lombard Street, Richardson Avenue, and Doyle Drive to Golden Gate Bridge—continue through Marin County via US 101 freeway. Exit at Sir Francis Drake Boulevard, in Larkspur; turn left. Take a left onto Center Boulevard in San Anselmo, followed by another left onto Fairfax-Bolinas Road; leave Fairfax. Take a left on Sky Oaks Road and follow it to Lake Lagunitas parking area ($8 fee as of this writing). *By public transit:* No transit service available. Starting point coordinates: 37.949653°N / 122.597539°W

The Ride

Easy mountain biking routes are rare in Marin County, except along trails adjacent to San Francisco Bay. The Mount Tamalpais environs are notoriously rugged and steep, as caused by uplifts along the San Andreas Fault and possibly other fault lines. The north slopes of Tamalpais are the gentlest; this is where Lap Lake Lagunitas is situated. Lap Lake

MOUNT TAMALPAIS WATERSHED

Lake Lagunitas is within protected lands of the Mount Tamalpais Watershed, as are nearby Alpine, Bon Tempe, Kent, and Phoenix Lakes. The west and east peaks of Mount Tamalpais are to the south; some debate exists as to which is taller, but 2,572 feet is the accepted maximum elevation. It is only the fifty-fifth-tallest peak in California, but Mount Tam's significance to the Bay Area must not be understated. In addition to the watershed, the Golden Gate National Recreation Areas, Mount Tamalpais State Park, Muir Woods National Monument, Point Reyes National Seashore (to the north), and several Marin County open spaces all combine to protect the mountain's diverse environments. Only a limited amount of low-density housing exists on the mountain's east and south sides. Paved roads encircle Tamalpais, at lower elevations, and climb to its peak, but most of the 115-square-mile space is accessible only by dirt fire roads and trails. Regarding those, Mount Tamalpais is recognized as a birthplace of mountain biking, during the late 1970s, when innovator-mechanic-athletes such as Gary Fisher and Joe Breeze took to the slopes on their newfangled contraptions. Downhill riding was their first pursuit. Some of those riders' performances can never be duplicated, as mountain bikes would later be banned from single-track trails to retain pristine environments. Riders can use the wider fire roads and trails, though, and the mountain is still an off-road mecca.

Lagunitas is a 6.35-mile barbell-shaped ride, including a 1.5-mile lap around Lake Lagunitas and a 1.8-mile loop north of Bon Tempe Lake. Other trails in the area feature either too much climbing to be considered "easy" or are off-limits to mountain bikes. The trails around nearby Bon Tempe Lake, for example, are for hikers and horses only. From the Lake Lagunitas parking area, head clockwise around the lake. The ride opens with a 300-foot-long stairway. After negotiating that, and the loop around the lake (mostly obscured by trees), return to the parking area, and continue north on Sky Oaks Road (paved), followed by a left on Bon Tempe Road, to begin another clockwise loop. This loop passes by the eastern corner of Alpine Lake and parallels Bon Tempe Creek for a stretch, along Bullfrog Fire Road. From there, the ride returns to Sky Oaks Road and then Lake Lagunitas.

Miles and Directions

0.0 Head south from the Lake Lagunitas parking area onto the fire road; begin climb (7.7% grade).

0.1 Fire road curves left, at east end of spillway; begin lake loop (note: 300-foot stairway).

0.25 Bear right to remain lakeside.

0.55 Stay right to remain lakeside; this is the highest elevation of the ride (810 feet).

1.05 Southeastern corner of lake; fire road curves right.

1.45 Keep straight at trail merge.

1.55 Keep straight at junction.

1.65 Curve right; follow trail downhill, back to the parking area.

1.75 Continue past parking area on Sky Oaks Road (paved).

2.0 Road curves left at Filter Plant Road.

2.3 Road curves right; Bon Tempe Lake at left (obscured by trees).

2.6 Keep straight at northeast corner of the lake; begin climb.

3.1 Left on Bon Tempe Road (dirt; net downhill).

3.6 Right on Bullfrog Fire Road (dirt).

4.0 Keep straight at Azalea Hill Trail junction; lowest elevation of the ride (660 feet).

4.4 Turn right to remain on Bullfrog Fire Road.

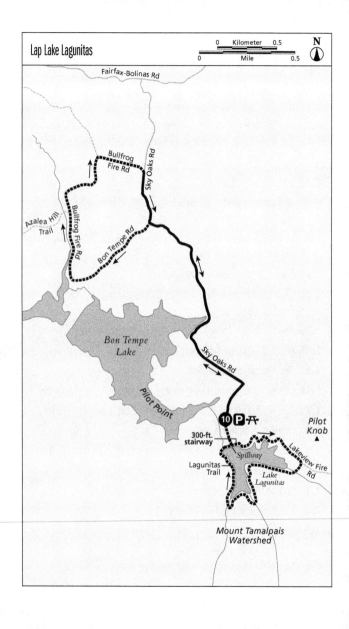

Lap Lake Lagunitas

Fairfax-Bolinas Rd

Bullfrog Fire Rd

Sky Oaks Rd

Azalea Hill Trail

Bullfrog Fire Rd

Bon Tempe Rd

Bon Tempe Lake

Pilot Point

Sky Oaks Rd

10 P ⛱

Pilot Knob ▲

300-ft. stairway

Lakeview Fire Rd

Lagunitas Trail

Spillway

Lake Lagunitas

Mount Tamalpais Watershed

N

Kilometer
0   0.5

Mile
0   0.5

4.6 End of the fire road; take right on Sky Oaks Road (adjacent to parking area, port a potties, and water), net climb to mile 5.3.

5.5 Bon Tempe Lake at right (obscured).

6.35 Arrive back at Lake Lagunitas parking area.

Bike Shops (Fairfax)

Krakatoa Bikes, 42 Bolinas Rd., (415) 453-0333, krakatoa bikes.net.

Sunshine Bicycle Center, 737 Center Blvd., (415) 459-3334, sunshinebicycle.com.

Best Easy

East Bay Rides

The East Bay is, perhaps, San Francisco's gateway to the California mainland. The East Bay offers the greatest opportunity for expansion; hence the greater proportion of the region's population is in the East Bay. The Oakland-Berkeley-Hayward urban division encompasses Alameda County and is one of three divisions that make up the San Francisco–Oakland–Berkeley metro area. Oakland is the second-largest city in the metro area. Despite having half the population of San Francisco—although it is larger by area—Oakland holds its own, as it boasts a major seaport, Oakland International Airport, professional sports teams, and thriving arts and music scenes. After crossing the Bay Bridge from San Francisco, Oakland becomes the gateway to cities to the north, such as Sacramento (state capital); east (all central California cities); and south (Fremont and San Jose), although the latter can be reached via the Peninsula. The University of California, Berkeley, is a stately educational and research institution that helps sustain the region's creativity, insight, and intelligence. Bicycling in the East Bay is diverse and varied, ranging from flat rides along the bay to hilly rides in the Berkeley Hills, within the Mount Diablo environs, and elsewhere. Oakland has been only a step behind San Francisco in terms of its accommodations for cyclists and pedestrians. Walk Oakland! has catalogued and mapped the city's walkways and alleys, plus the bike routes and lanes. And there is a local website that features photos of stolen bicycles to assist victims in identifying and finding their wheels. Eleven East Bay rides follow, including ones in Alameda, Fremont, Lafayette, Martinez, Oakland, Richmond, San Leandro, and Union City.

11 Around Alameda

Start: Washington Park, 740 Central Ave., Alameda
Length: 10.9 miles (counter-clockwise loop)
Riding time: 40 to 120 minutes (my time: 50:49)
Terrain and surface: 59 percent paved roads, 40 percent paved paths, 1 percent walkways
Elevations: Low—1 foot on the bike path adjacent to Robert W.

Crown Memorial State Beach (southeast end); high—17 feet on the bike path west and south of Atlantic Avenue
Daily traffic volumes: Traffic volume data unavailable.
Map: *The Thomas Guide by Rand McNally—Street Guide: Alameda County* (any recent year), page 669

Getting there: *By car:* From central San Francisco, cross the Bay Bridge (I-80), entering Oakland. Exit to I-980 South; transfer to I-880 South. Exit to Alameda via the Webster Tube (CA 61). Enter Alameda on Webster Street. Turn left on Central Avenue, then right on 8th Street. Parking for Washington Park is at right. *By public transit:* From central San Francisco, ride AC Transit bus route W from the Transbay Terminal to Washington Park during commute hours (p.m. only to Alameda, a.m. only to San Francisco). At other times, ride the Alameda Ferry from the San Francisco Ferry Terminal to Alameda's terminal. Transfer to AC Transit bus route 63, which stops at Washington Park. Route 63 runs every half hour daily. Starting point coordinates: 37.767964°N / 122.272697°W

The Ride

Alameda is probably the flattest city in the Bay Area, making it ideal for a nonhilly ride. Most of Alameda occupies Alameda Island (see sidebar), making a perimeter ride logical. Putting the two together, Around Alameda is a 10.9-mile road ride around the main island. The route drifts away from the perimeter, though, in part because through travel along the shoreline is not possible. The ride starts at Washington Park, then heads to the island's west coast, adjacent to Robert W. Crown Memorial State Beach. What was formerly Neptune Beach became a state park in 1959. It was later renamed in honor of California Assemblyman Robert W. Crown. Although it is a state beach, it is operated by the East Bay Regional Park District. After a long stretch adjacent to

ALAMEDA

The city of Alameda occupies two islands—Alameda and Bay Farm (Harbor Bay)—in San Francisco Bay. The estimated population was 78,300 in 2018, up 7 percent since 2010. Harbor Bay Island is connected to the mainland; Alameda Island originally was, too, but became separated after dredging for nearby Oakland International Airport removed and relocated some land. Before being developed, a large portion of Alameda, extending into nearby downtown Oakland, was coastal oak forest. It is hard to envision today, although the area's original name, Encinal, means "forest of evergreen oak," and, Alameda means "grove of trees" or "tree lined." The name was chosen in 1853 after its founding that year by Euro-Americans. The new city combined three settlements: Alameda, Hibbardsville, and Woodstock. Notable milestones in Alameda's history include the arrival of the first transcontinental train in September 1869—the terminus was moved to Oakland just two months later. Neptune Beach, an amusement park, was built along the bay shore in 1917. The park remained popular until 1939, when hardships of the Great Depression were keeping people away. Also, the completion of the Bay Bridge had changed travel patterns. The Alameda Naval Air Station was built in 1941 and was in service until 1997. As for pop culture, scenes from *The Matrix* film trilogy were shot in Alameda, including the bullet-dodging sequences.

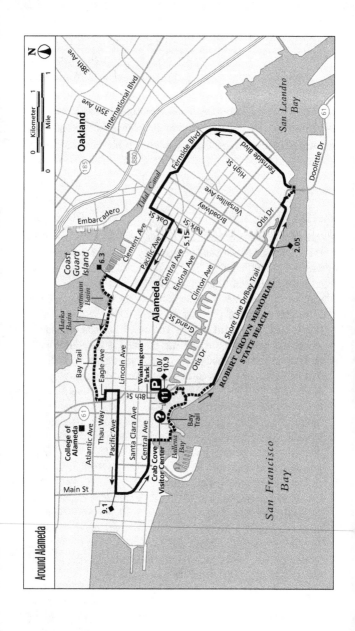

Around Alameda

the beach, the route turns to pass through neighborhoods. Victorian-era houses are common. On the island's east side, the route passes Fortmann Basin, the Fortmann Marina, and the Encinal Terminals, using the Bay Trail. After leaving the shore area, the ride heads west, then north, through more neighborhoods. The route misses the northern part of the island entirely; that area, now known as Alameda Point, is the former home of the Alameda Naval Air Station. The ride ends with another shoreline stretch.

Miles and Directions

0.0 From the Washington Park parking area, head south on the walkway adjacent to 8th Avenue.

0.15 Right on connector path (head toward shoreline).

0.25 Leave circle, continue onto adjacent path (southward).

0.35 Sand Castle picnic area at right.

0.6 Path now adjacent to Shoreline Drive (on left) and Robert Crown Memorial State Beach (at right).

2.05 Path curves left; now on walkway adjacent to Broadway.

2.1 Leave walkway; right on Bayview Drive, ride in road.

2.45 Bayview curves left.

2.5 Traffic signal at Otis Drive; turn right.

2.6 Leave Otis Drive to right via bike path.

2.65 Path crosses Peach Street.

2.7 Turn right to continue on path.

2.75 Path curves left and passes under Otis Drive.

2.85 Merge onto two-way bike lane adjacent to Fernside Boulevard.

3.05 End two-way bike lane at San Jose Avenue; continue in road (Fernside Boulevard).

3.2 Traffic signals at Encinal Avenue, Central Avenue (mile 3.35), and Liberty Avenue (mile 3.45); keep straight at each inter-section.

3.5 Stop sign at Eastshore Avenue; keep straight.

3.95 Traffic signal at High Street; keep straight.

4.4 Traffic signal at Fruitvale Avenue; keep straight, now on Blanding Avenue.

4.5 Stop sign at Broadway; keep straight.

4.75 Traffic signal at Park Street; keep straight.

4.85 Road bends 90 degrees left; now on Oak Street.

4.95 Stop sign at Clement Avenue; keep straight.

5.05 Traffic signal at Buena Vista Avenue; keep straight.

5.15 Right on Pacific Avenue.

5.3 Stop signs at Walnut Street, Willow Street (mile 5.5), Schiller Street (mile 5.8), and Union Street (mile 5.85); keep straight at each intersection.

5.95 Stop sign at Grand Street; turn right.

6.0 Traffic signal at Buena Vista Avenue; keep straight.

6.3 Left onto bike path; marina at right.

6.5 Path bends 90 degrees left, then 90 degrees right (note: there were some unimproved path segments as of this writing).

6.7 Bear left, then right through the parking area adjacent to Marina Cove Waterfront Park; continue onto path.

7.05 Leave path; take left onto short connector, then left onto Atlantic Avenue walkway.

7.1 Turn right to cross Atlantic Avenue; continue onto short connector, then right onto bike path.

7.75 End of path; left onto Atlantic Avenue walkway, then left onto Constitution Parkway walkway.

7.8 Leave Constitution Parkway; bear left then right to access Thau Way.

7.85 Stop sign at Eagle Avenue; turn left.

7.95 Stop sign at 8th Street; turn right.

8.05 Stop sign at Buena Vista Avenue; keep straight.

8.1 Right on Pacific Avenue.

8.15 Traffic signals at Constitution Parkway and Webster Street (mile 8.3); keep straight at each intersection.

8.4 Stop signs at 5th Street and Marshall Way (mile 8.75); keep straight at each intersection.

8.95 Traffic signal at 3rd Street; keep straight.

9.1 Traffic signal at Central Avenue; turn left.

9.6 Traffic signal at Ballena Boulevard; keep straight.

9.8 Stop sign at 5th Street; keep straight.

9.85 Right onto paved path (just east of Hoover Place).

9.9 Shoreline at right.

10.5 Crab Cove at left.

10.65 Left onto connector path.

10.75 Left onto path to return to park.

10.9 Arrive back at the Washington Park parking area.

Bike Shops (Alameda)

Alameda Bicycle, 1522 Park St., (510) 522-0070, alameda bicycle.com

Cycle City, 1433 High St., (510) 521-2872, cyclecityusa.com

Island City Bicycles, 2427 Clement Ave., (510) 418-1552, islandcitybicycles.com

Stone's Cyclery, 2320 Santa Clara Ave., (510) 523-3264, stonescyclery.com

Westside Joe's Bikes, 1000 Central Ave., (510) 995-8582

Zach Kaplan Cycles, 1518 Buena Vista Ave., (510) 522-2368, zachkaplancycles.com

12 Briones: Bovine to Equine

Start: Briones Regional Park: Alhambra Creek Staging Area
Length: 4.1 miles (counterclockwise loop)
Riding time: 30 to 65 minutes (my time: 1H01:59, on foot)
Terrain and surface: 62 percent dirt trails and roads, 30 percent paved roads, 8 percent paved path

Elevations: Low—217 feet at Reliez Valley and Tavan Estates Roads; high—579 feet on Hidden Pond Trail west of Sunrise Ridge Drive
Traffic and hazards: Traffic volume data unavailable.
Map: *The Thomas Guide by Rand McNally—Street Guide: Contra Costa County* (any recent year), page 591

Getting there: *By car*: From central San Francisco, cross the Bay Bridge (I-80), entering Oakland. Transfer to I-580, and then to I-980 (CA 24). Enter Contra Costa County after passing through the Caldecott Tunnel. Exit at Pleasant Hill Road (loop ramp) and head north. Turn left on Reliez Valley Road. Once in Martinez, look for the Alhambra Creek Staging Area entrance to Briones Regional Park on the left. Travel the entry road (Brookwood Road) to parking (entry fee). *By public transit*: From central San Francisco, ride BART to Concord. Transfer to County Connection bus route 16, which travels between Concord BART and Martinez. Exit the bus at Alhambra Avenue and Blue Ridge Drive. Ride west on Blue Ridge, right on Reliez Valley Road, and left on Brookwood Road (Alhambra Valley entrance to Briones Regional Park). Route 16 runs every 40 minutes on weekdays only, but is free(!). BART trains to Concord run every 15 minutes on weekdays and Sunday, and every 20 minutes on Saturday. Starting point coordinates: 37.956683°N / 122.123167°W

The Ride

Briones Regional Park occupies a large expanse of land (4,202 acres) in the Briones Hills, sandwiched between urbanized Alameda and Contra Costa Counties to the west, and the Concord UZA to the east. Watershed land that was formerly owned by the East Bay Municipal Utilities District (EBMUD) was gradually taken over by the East Bay Regional Park District starting in 1966, turning the hills into recreational space. (EBMUD lands to the west and northwest are also recreational, but require a permit.) The park is large enough to have three separate entrances. This ride uses the northeast entrance, in the city of Martinez. The park is hilly, topped by Briones Peak (elevation 1,484

OPEN RANGE

The notion of sharing a trail with or passing near grazing cattle should not be alarming. Despite their size, cattle are vegetarians and more fearful of you on your bicycle than you are of them. Common sense would be to slow down when near cattle and to avoid excessive noise. Open-range practices date back to the nineteenth century. It is likely that the United States imported the concept from Mexico. Open range is strictly a western United States phenomenon, though—laws in the eastern United States restrict cattle to herds and fenced-in, privately owned areas. The practice is more necessary in the West, though, because water can be scattered over wide areas, or even scarce. Barbed wire was prevalent as a way to separate grazing from developed land in the late nineteenth century. That practice has been banned, although one may find remnants of old barbed-wire fencing in remote areas. You won't see any barbs in Briones; cattle are confined by simple wooden fencing and gates that humans can easily open and shut.

feet). Briones: Bovine to Equine is as gentle as a ride can get here, despite a cumulative 670 feet of climbing. The climbs are separated by downhills, though. The 4.1-mile mountain bike ride stays within the northeastern sector of the park, where the hills are relatively tame. The ride title refers to a share-the-trail philosophy in which the route passes through open range (bovine), and adjacent to a stable (equine). After opening with a climb to a ridge, the ride descends into the adjacent neighborhood, for an on-road stretch. The ride reenters the park, climbing to a different hilltop, then enters an open range. The trail can be bumpy and uneven here, with moguls that develop from hoof depressions made when the ground is soft, such as after a rain. After passing a stable, the route returns to the starting point along a trail that parallels the park entry road.

Miles and Directions

0.0 Start from the Alhambra Creek Staging Area at Briones Regional Park; enter the gate and turn left on Orchard Trail.

0.1 Right on Diablo View Trail; begin climb to ridge (13.9% grade).

0.3 Crest of ridge; bear left on Hidden Pond Trail; descend (9.9% grade), then climb (11.0% grade).

0.6 Highest elevation of ride (579 feet); begin descent.

0.7 Leave trail and enter residential area; now on Sunrise Ridge Drive.

1.05 Left on Hidden Pond Road; descend (12.4% grade).

1.5 Stop sign at Reliez Valley Road; cross road to access parallel paved path; turn left.

1.8 Turn left and leave path; cross Reliez Valley Road to access Tavan Estates Drive; this is the lowest elevation of the ride (217 feet).

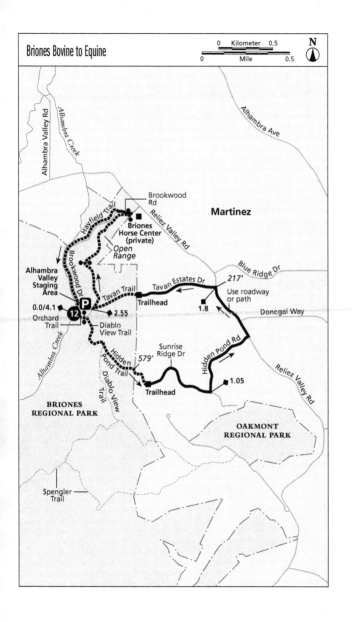

Briones Bovine to Equine

Kilometer 0.5

Mile 0.5

N

Alhambra Valley Rd

Alhambra Creek

Alhambra Ave

Hayfield Trail

Brookwood Rd

Reliez Valley Rd

Martinez

Briones Horse Center (private)

Open Range

Brookwood Dr

Alhambra Valley Staging Area

Tavan Trail

Tavan Estates Dr

Tavan Trail Trailhead

Blue Ridge Dr

217'

Use roadway or path

Donegal Way

0.0/4.1

12 P

2.55

Orchard Trail

Diablo View Trail

1.8

Hidden Pond Trail

579'

Sunrise Ridge Dr

Hidden Pond Rd

Reliez Valley Rd

Trailhead

1.05

Diablo View Trail

Alhambra Creek

BRIONES REGIONAL PARK

OAKMONT REGIONAL PARK

Spengler Trail

2.25 End of road; keep straight onto Tavan Trail; continue climb (5.3% grade).

2.55 Sharp right onto unnamed trail; continue climb (8.7% grade).

2.7 Crest of climb (elevation 487 feet); begin gradual descent.

2.8 Gate; enter open range area; it's a bumpy trail and cattle may be present.

3.25 End of open range, adjacent to stable; pass through gate and cross Brookwood Road.

3.3 Continue onto Hayfield Trail, parallel to Brookwood Road.

3.7 Trail nearly merges with road.

4.0 End trail; continue through parking area (dirt).

4.1 Arrive back at the staging area and gate.

Bike Shops (Pleasant Hill)

Big Dave's Bikes, 609 Gregory Ln., #120, (925) 954-1956, bigdavesbikes.com

Frame Up Bikes, 181 Mayhew Way #D, (925) 433-5910, frameupbikes.com

13 Garbage Mountain Bayside Mush

Start: North Richmond Ballfield Complex, 3rd Street (Fred Jackson Way) and Da Villa, Richmond
Length: 6.0 miles (lollipop with counterclockwise loop).
Riding time: 30 to 80 minutes (my time: 34:52)
Terrain and surface: 74 percent dirt & compacted aggregate trails, 24 percent paved paths, 2 percent concrete walkway

Elevations: Low—3 feet in tidal area south of Garbage Mountain; high—13 feet at North Richmond Ballfield
Daily traffic volumes: 100 percent of the ride is off-road
Map: The Thomas Guide by Rand McNally—Street Guide: Contra Costa County (any recent year), page 588

Getting there: By car: From central San Francisco, cross the Bay Bridge (I-80), entering Oakland. Continue on I-80 to Richmond. Exit at San Pablo Dam Road; turn left. Turn right on Evans Avenue; merge onto San Pablo Avenue. Turn left on Church Lane; the road becomes Market Avenue. Turn right on 3rd Street—North Richmond Ballfield will be on the right. By public transit: From central San Francisco, ride BART (Bay Area Rapid Transit) to Richmond. Transfer to AC Transit bus route 76. Exit the bus at Filbert Street and Market Avenue, one block from the ballfield. Route 76 runs every half hour on weekdays, and hourly on weekends. BART trains to Richmond run every 15 minutes on weekdays, and every 20 minutes on Saturday. On Sunday, a train transfer in Oakland is required. Starting point coordinates: 37.961083°N / 122.366675°W

The Ride

Garbage Mountain Bayside Mush, at first read, may sound like a grotesque ride through a trash pile, complete with odors and toxicity. Contrarily, the route is a pleasant outing—

GARBAGE MOUNTAIN

Contrary to its name, you won't see any trash at Garbage Mountain. As is customary with landfills, the trash has been compacted and buried over the years. Once a landfill reaches capacity, then the overlying surface slowly returns to a natural state. The garbage remains underground, though, and must be decontaminated and contained. Garbage Mountain is now open to the public after years of settlement and remediation. For decades, landfills have been the number one trash repository in the United States. One look at Garbage Mountain suggests a potential problem: What to do when the landfill reaches capacity? About 90 percent of US landfills were completely full by the 1990s. This mandated a more serious consideration of other options, including incineration, ocean dumping, bioremediation, and recycling. Each of these has advantages and disadvantages. But, when the mountain can go no higher, an alternative is clearly needed.

surprisingly—along Wildcat Creek and San Pablo Bay, in northern Richmond. A former landfill that reached capacity has been converted into recreational space. The ride starts at the North Richmond Ball Park (entry was closed when I did this ride; I parked on Fred Jackson Way). The route immediately heads west on Wildcat Creek Trail (paved). The passage under Richmond Parkway was flooded when I did this during the winter, but was dry—yet messy—when I did it during the summer; the bypass route involved leaving the path to cross the parkway at grade and then entering the Wildcat Marsh Staging Area. (The ride could be staged here, but the longer version gets to use a segment of Wildcat Creek Trail.) After leaving the trailhead, Wildcat Creek Trail bends to the right to become Wildcat Marsh Trail. From here, trail surfaces vary between compacted aggregate, graded dirt, and

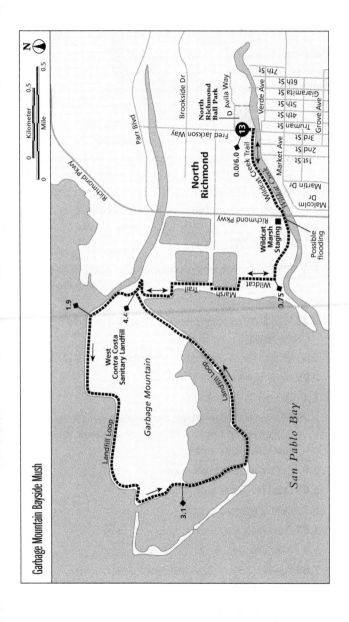

Garbage Mountain Bayside Mush

N

0   0.5   Kilometer   0.5
0   Mile

Richmond Pkwy

Parr Blvd

Brookside Dr

North Richmond

Fred Jackson Way

North Richmond Ball Park

D Avila Way

13 0.0/6.0

Wildcat Creek Trail

Verde Ave

7th St
6th St   Giaramita St
5th St
4th St
3rd St   Truman St   Grove Ave
2nd St
1st St   Market Ave

Malcolm Dr   Martin Dr

Wildcat Creek

Richmond Pkwy

Wildcat Marsh Staging

Possible flooding

Wildcat Marsh Trail

0.75

1.9

West Contra Costa Sanitary Landfill

4.4

Garbage Mountain

Landfill Loop

Landfill Loop

3.1

San Pablo Bay

some short paved segments. Follow the signage to remain on the correct trail. After passing the landfill's entrance—it still accepts certain items—the ride begins a counterclockwise loop around Garbage Mountain. The trail is bayside (San Pablo Bay) for a long stretch, and then it passes through marshlands and tidelands. From a distance, the trail appears to disappear into the bay, but rest assured that it is a through route. But, it can be a wet environment, with some mud and puddles. Near the end of the loop, signage explains the transformation of Garbage Mountain. After closing the loop, the ride returns to the North Richmond Ballfield.

Miles and Directions

0.0 Start at North Richmond Ball Park; head south on Fred Jackson Way, then turn right, crossing the street, onto Wildcat Creek Trail (paved).

0.45 Pass under Richmond Parkway (flooded when I did this during the winter).

0.5 Wildcat Marsh Staging Area; continue on Wildcat Creek Trail.

0.75 Right on Wildcat Marsh Trail.

1.1 Trail bends right then left.

1.25 Trail bends 90 degrees left, then 90 degrees right (mile 1.35), 90 degrees right (mile 1.45), and two 90-degree lefts in succession (mile 1.55).

1.6 Begin counterclockwise loop.

1.65 Cross Parr Boulevard/Garden Tract Road.

1.7 Landfill entrance at right.

1.75 Cross road.

1.9 Trail curves left.

2.05 San Pablo Bay at right; trail curves along bayside.

3.1 Trail junction; keep straight onto spit; enter tidelands area.

3.4 Trail curves left.

4.05 Keep straight at junction; note intermittent signage at left.

4.4 End of loop; right onto Wildcat Marsh Trail.

4.45 Stay on trail as it executes a series of 90-degree bends (reverse of outbound route).

5.25 End of Wildcat Marsh Trail; left on Wildcat Creek Trail.

5.5 Pass Wildcat Marsh Staging Area.

5.55 Pass under Richmond Parkway (if not flooded).

5.95 Cross Fred Jackson Way; turn left.

6.0 Arrive back at North Richmond Ball Park.

Bike Shops (Richmond)

Cycology Bicycle Company, 120 MacDonald Ave., #206, (415) 846-7352, repairs.

Rich City Rides, 1500 MacDonald Ave., (510) 900-1799, richcityrides.org.

14 Get to the Point Richmond

Start: Judge George D. Carroll Park, Cutting and Garrard Boulevards, Richmond

Length: 5.9 miles (clockwise loop with an out-and-back segment)

Riding time: 25 to 75 minutes (my time: 1H05:08 on foot)

Terrain and surface: 93 percent paved paths and concrete walkways, 7 percent paved roads

Elevations: Low—4 feet adjacent to Miller-Knox Lagoon; high—37 feet at Garrard Boulevard Tunnel portal

Traffic and hazards: The daily traffic volume on Camino Capistrano near Northwest Open Space was 6,000.

Map: *The Thomas Guide by Rand McNally—Street Guide: Contra Costa County* (any recent year), page 608

Getting there: *By car:* From central San Francisco, cross the Bay Bridge (I-80), entering Oakland. Continue on I-80 to Richmond; transfer to I-580, toward San Rafael. Exit at Canal Boulevard; turn left. Turn right on Cutting Boulevard, then left on Vine Street, and right on Richmond Avenue. Carroll Park will be on the right. *By public transit:* From central San Francisco, ride BART to Richmond. Transfer to AC transit bus route 72M. Exit the bus at Garrard Boulevard and Richmond Avenue, adjacent to Carroll Park. Route 72M runs daily every 30 to 40 minutes. Starting point coordinates: 37.924553°N / 122.383542°W

The Ride

Get to the Point Richmond is a 5.9-mile road ride that soaks in the transformed shoreline of Point Richmond (see sidebar). The ride visits a portion of the industrial waterfront, which has historical character, and the modern waterfront community of Brickyard Cove. The route misses the Point Richmond Historic District, but a visit there is

POINT RICHMOND

Point Richmond is located in the southwestern corner of Richmond, just southeast of the Richmond–San Rafael Bridge, along the San Francisco Bay-front. The Point, which is a vibrant community, is dominated by Nicholl Knob, which juts upward with steep slopes. (There were formerly several "knobs" between Richmond and Berkeley, but most of them have been detonated.) The community is easy to miss, given that it is bordered by industrial and port activities that would seem to be incompatible with residential life. Residents do complain about freight train noise but concurrently work to preserve historical railroad infrastructure. Point Richmond was the city of Richmond's central district until the early twentieth century. Today Nicholl Knob divides Point Richmond into a historic district that is on the National Register of Historic Places and a modern waterfront community. Miller-Knox Regional Shoreline bridges the two communities, complete with a lake and beach.

recommended. The ride starts at Judge George D. Carroll Park—Judge Carroll served in WWII and was the first black lawyer in Richmond. He was also Richmond's first black mayor and served on the Bay Municipal Court for twenty years. After a gritty start to the ride, with a segment along Cutting Boulevard, and an active railroad crossing on Canal Boulevard, the route moves to Shipyard 3 Trail, which is a paved path. Signage along the way provides interpretive information. The ride continues beyond the trail's junction with the Ferry Point Loop Trail, to a dead end at the Point Potrero Marine Terminal. Immediately to the east, on the opposite side of Harbor Channel, is the Rosie the Riveter National Historic Site. The route returns to Ferry Point Loop Trail, then continues along the waterfront, through the Brickyard Cove community. Despite the urban context, I saw three deer wander across a road here. The ride then enters Miller-Knox Regional Shoreline, passing near Keller Beach. From there, after a short climb, the ride takes aim at Nicholl Knob, passing right through it via the Garrard Boulevard Tunnel (also known as Ferry Point Tunnel, Point Richmond Tunnel, and Dornan Drive Tunnel). The tunnel was built in 1912 and is 741 feet long (it will seem longer once inside). After exiting the tunnel, it is a straight shot to Carroll Park.

Miles and Directions

0.0 From Judge George D. Carroll Park, head east on Richmond Avenue.

0.2 Left on Wine Street.

0.4 Right on Cutting Boulevard, after railroad crossing—narrow shoulder.

0.45 Traffic signal at Canal Boulevard; turn right; skewed railroad crossing after turn.

1.1 Begin designated bike path (Shipyard 3 Trail) on right, parallel to road.

1.15 Cross Seacliff Drive; keep straight.

1.4 Trail parking at right.

1.65 Trail to Observation Point at right.

1.7 Trail curves right, then left.

2.3 Trail junction; begin out-and-back segment—cross Canal Boulevard and turn right to continue on Shipyard 3 Trail.

2.6 Trail executes a series of 90-degree bends.

2.9 Final 90-degree bend; continue to end of path.

3.0 End path at waterfront; turn around here.

3.7 Return to trail junction; cross Canal Boulevard and continue via Ferry Point Loop Trail (paved path).

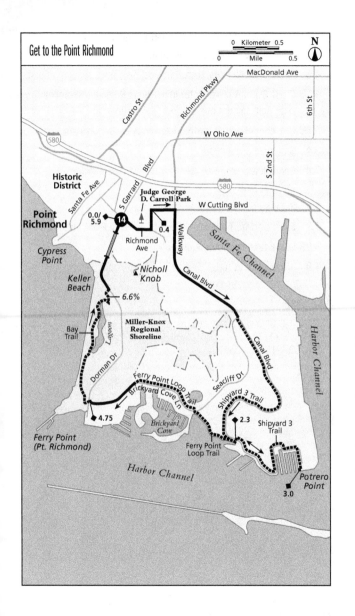

Get to the Point Richmond

0 — Kilometer — 0.5
0 — Mile — 0.5

N

MacDonald Ave

Castro St

Richmond Pkwy

W Ohio Ave

S 6th St

S 2nd St

580

Historic District

Santa Fe Ave

S Garrard Blvd

Judge George D. Carroll Park

580

W Cutting Blvd

Point Richmond

0.0/ 5.9

14

Richmond Ave

0.4

Walkway

Santa Fe Channel

Cypress Point

Nicholl Knob

Canal Blvd

Keller Beach

6.6%

Canal Blvd

Bay Trail

Lagoon

Miller-Knox Regional Shoreline

Harbor Channel

Dorman Dr

Ferry Point Loop Trail

Brickyard Cove Ln

Seacliff Dr

Shipyard 3 Trail

4.75

Brickyard Cove

2.3

Shipyard 3 Trail

Ferry Point (Pt. Richmond)

Ferry Point Loop Trail

Potrero Point

3.0

Harbor Channel

4.05 Cross Seacliff Drive and turn left to continue on trail; now adjacent to Brickyard Cove Lane.

4.3 Cross Brick Kiln Way, then Brickyard Way; keep straight on path.

4.75 Cross Dornan Drive; enter Miller-Knox Regional Shoreline; bear right to continue on Ferry Point Loop Trail.

5.05 Left to continue on path; Miller-Knox Lagoon at right.

5.4 Stay right at junction.

5.45 Sharp left onto path; veer right, uphill (6.6% grade), to leave park.

5.6 Pathway now adjacent to Dornan Drive.

5.7 Enter Garrard Tunnel (also known as Ferry Point Tunnel).

5.85 Leave tunnel; continue on walkway.

5.9 Arrive back at Judge George D. Carroll Park.

Bike Shop

Litton Cycles, 999 West Cutting Blvd., #15, Richmond, (510) 237–1132, repairs.

15 Treasure (Island) Hunt

Start: Middle Harbor Shoreline Park, 2777 Middle Harbor Road, Oakland

Length: 11.4 miles (turn around at end of bridge path on Yerba Buena Island) or 16.4 miles (out-and-back with short loop around Treasure Island)

Riding time: 45 minutes to 2½ hours (my times: 51:05 for short option; 1H16:42 for long option)

Terrain and surface: 100 percent paved roads (note that there are paths that parallel roads on Treasure Island)

Elevations: Low—sea level in Treasure Island's residential area; high—224 feet on Treasure Island Road, on Yerba Buena Island

Daily traffic volumes: Treasure Island traffic volume data unavailable.

Map: *The Thomas Guide by Rand McNally—Street Guide: Alameda County* (any recent year), page 649

Getting there: *By car:* From central San Francisco, cross the Bay Bridge (I-80). Exit to I-880 southbound. Exit at Union Street; turn left on 7th Street. Turn left on Middle Harbor Road, then right into Middle Harbor Shoreline Park. *By public transit:* From central San Francisco, ride BART to West Oakland. From the station, head west on 7th Street. Turn left on Middle Harbor Road, then right into Middle Harbor Shoreline Park. Starting point coordinates: 37.806206°N / 122.332478°W

The Ride

Treasure (Island) Hunt should be on your bucket list, as crossing the Bay Bridge on a bicycle is now feasible. It is not possible to cross the entire bridge, but the stretch from Oakland to Yerba Buena Island, via the Alex Zuckermann Path, has been completed in conjunction with the reconstruction of that portion of the bridge. The path is open every day from 6 a.m. to 9 p.m. (nighttime riding is prohibited). The

TREASURE ISLAND

Treasure Island—not to be confused with Robert Louis Stevenson's fantasy thriller—is an artificial island in San Francisco Bay. The all-flat island has an area of 0.9 square mile and adjoins Yerba Buena Island, which is natural. Treasure Island (TI) was completed in time for the 1939 Golden Gate International Exposition, which was held there. It was a busy time, as both the Golden Gate and Bay Bridges had been completed just a few years earlier. TI was a "Magic Isle," with large courtyards and exhibit halls. The island was not a folly, though—shallow underwater shoals previously were a shipping hazard, and protection was sensible. The post-Exposition plan was to convert TI into an auxiliary airport, to supplement San Francisco International, but WWII intervened. TI subsequently became a naval air station that was active until 1997. Today, essentially all of TI's buildings, and the island itself, are on the National Register of Historic Places. The island's residences are occupied by private citizens; TI has an estimated population of 2,600. Plans are for a population of 19,000, although one may wonder where they are all going to fit in less than 1 square mile(!). Yerba Buena Island, in contrast, is rugged, with steep hillsides that plunge into the Bay. The US Coast Guard maintains a presence there.

11.4-mile option travels from the Port of Oakland to Vista Point on Yerba Buena Island, and back. The 16.4-mile route extends this with 13.65 miles of out-and-back riding, plus a 2.75-mile lap around Treasure Island. The ride begins at Middle Harbor Shoreline Park in far western Oakland, within that city's port environment. There is a bike path all the way to the Bay Bridge, with at-grade crossings. Regarding that, the Port of Oakland teems with trucks and freight trains. Even though the bike path is separated from the roads, it is imperative to be cautious at all road and driveway crossings. There are a few railroad crossings, too. The opening segment

Treasure (Island) Hunt

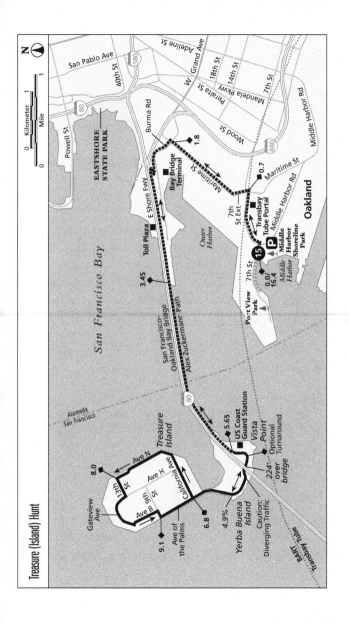

of the path passes the Transbay Tube portal, where BART trains emerge from and initiate their underwater crossings of the Bay. The bridge segment is 3.5 miles, of which 2.2 miles is over water. Once on the Bay Bridge, Zuckermann Path begins to elevate. By the time the bridge reaches Yerba Buena Island, you are 183 feet above the water. Immediately to the left, at the end of the path on Yerba Buena Island, is Vista Point. From here, shuttles transport cyclists to Treasure Island. It is a convenient, free service for those who are not up to conquering the 5 percent gradient uphill and downhill on Hillcrest and Treasure Island Roads. Although these roads are narrow and curvy, they are designated as shared facilities. The shuttle bus runs every half hour on weekends and holidays, from 7 a.m. to 6:30 p.m. Treasure Island is pancake flat, and the 2.75-mile loop is easy-breezy. The Treasure Island Museum at right greets you at the start of the loop. Roads on the island were rough and damaged when I rode this (summer 2020), though, Major construction was underway, with some effects on roads. Paths (not shown on the map) could be used to bypass construction in some places.

Miles and Directions

0.0 Exit Middle Harbor Shoreline Park via the path on the northeast side—cross Middle Harbor Drive (watch for moving and queued trucks).

0.05 Bear left onto 7th Street bike path (parallel to 7th Street).

0.5 BART Transbay Tube portal at left.

0.7 Traffic signal at 7th Street Extension; cross road, then cross 7th Street; path now parallel to 7th Street Extension.

0.9 Path curves right; now parallel to Maritime Street.

1.3 Traffic signal at entry point (also at mile 1.5).

1.8 Traffic signal at Burma Road; cross Burma, then cross Maritime Street; path now parallel to Burma.

2.0 Railroad crossing.

2.05 Railroad crossing (four tracks, three skewed), as path curves left.

2.15 Path curves right then left.

2.2 Left on Bay Bridge Trail (Alex Zuckermann Path), under freeway structure.

2.6 Bay Bridge Toll Plaza at right (no bicycle toll).

3.45 Path and bridge begin to elevate; now over water.

5.65 Path leaves bridge; exiting to Yerba Buena Island.

5.7 Enter Hillcrest Road and begin climb (4.6% grade); Vista Point at left (option to ride shuttle to Treasure Island, or turn around here).

5.95 Highest elevation of ride (224 feet), on Treasure Island Road, directly over I-80; begin curving descent.

6.7 Enter Treasure Island; Treasure Island Museum at right

6.8 Right on California Avenue (4th Street); begin counterclockwise loop (construction detour from Treasure Island Road: right on Clipper Cove Way or waterfront path, left on Clipper Way, then right on California).

7.0 Stop sign at Avenue D; keep straight.

7.3 Left on Avenue N (edge of island; or use Avenue M).

8.0 Left on 13th Street.

8.1 Stop sign at Avenue M; keep straight.

8.25 Stop sign at Gateview Avenue; turn right. Enter residential area (lowest elevation of the ride: sea level).

8.7 Left on Avenue B.

9.0 Stop sign at 9th Street; turn right.

9.1 Road curves 90 degrees left; now on Avenue of the Palms (or use parallel waterfront path).

9.55 Return to California Avenue/4th Street; end of loop; begin climb (4.9% grade) on Treasure Island Road.

10.25 Caution: on-ramp to Bay Bridge; diverging vehicles.

10.4 Crest of climb (elevation 224 feet) over I-80; begin descent (now on Hillcrest Road).

10.7 Bear right onto Alex Zuckermann Path; use caution.

12.9 End of bridge; path now on land.

14.15 Leave Zuckermann Path; right on path to Port.

(Note that the return ride description omits details.)

14. 5 Left onto path adjacent to Maritime Street.

15.45 Path curves left; now adjacent to 7th Street Extension.

15.65 Traffic signal at 7th Street; cross street and turn right onto 7th Street Path.

16.4 Arrive back at Middle Harbor Shoreline Park; return to parking.

Bike Shops (Oakland)

Archer Bicycle, 413 13th St., (510) 681-1141, repairs
Bikes 4 Life, 1600 7th St., (510) 452-2453, bikes4life.com
King Kog Bicycle Shop, 327 17th St., (510) 858-7514, kingkog.bigcartel.com

Honorable Mention

The following are ten additional easy San Francisco rides. Space limitations prohibited the inclusion of map and mileage logs for these. The text describes each route.

16 A Spin Through Glen Canyon

What: 2.1-mile mountain bike ride (San Francisco). **Stage:** Glen Park Recreation Center, 70 Elk St., San Francisco (37.736233°N / 122.439919°W). **Elevation differential:** 314 feet. **Route:** Narrow clockwise loop with a short middle "neck," heading north from Glen Park Recreation Center via Islais Creek Trail (westernmost trail) on west side of Islais Creek. Continue climbing to unnamed connector trail near Portola Drive (stairs near top), right on connector to Amethyst Street, Turquoise Way, right on connector 0.15 mile south of Amethyst (stairs), south on outbound trail, then stay left to ride on east side of canyon (Coyote Crags Trail— rugged segments). At fork, stay right, leaving Coyote Crags, to remain in canyon—now on Gum Tree Girls Trail. Return to Recreation Center.

17 Bair Island to Bayfront

What: 8.15-mile road ride (Redwood City). **Stage:** Sam-Trans Park and Ride Lot, 162 Veterans Blvd., Redwood City (37.494889°N / 122.234489°W). **Elevation differential:** 11 feet. **Route:** Out-and-back with a short loop at the turnaround. From park and ride lot via Veterans Boulevard (use walkway; cross Whipple Avenue), Turn left to ride in designated bike lane in center of Whipple. Cross Bayshore

Road to Bay Trail (turn right; partially paved path), Bair Island Road (right), circle at Bayshore Road, exit left to path, "Bridge to Nowhere" (steep lip at end of bridge), path (dirt segments), Maple Street (left), Blomquist Street (left), Seaport Boulevard (left; parallel path on east side), right on path near end of Seaport (begin loop), enter road (Seaport Boulevard) when path is adjacent, continue on Seaport to end of loop, then return via reverse of outbound route.

18 Coyote Hills Untamed

What: 6.8-mile mountain bike ride (Fremont). **Stage:** Coyote Hills Regional Park, Quarry Staging Area, 8000 Patterson Ranch Rd., Fremont (37.551375°N / 122.085625°W). **Elevation differential:** 53 feet. **Route:** Clockwise loop. Head south from Quarry Staging Area parking via Bayview Trail (paved), left on unnamed dirt connector, Bayview Trail (circumnavigates hills on the right), Chochenyo Trail (left turn opposite Visitor Center), straight onto D.U.S.T. Trail, merge onto Alameda Creek Trail, sharp right near Ardenwood Boulevard to Crandall Creek Trail (route avoids often-flooded trail connector), curve left to Willows Trail, right on Chochenyo Trail, left on Muskrat Trail, cross road to Bayview Trail, end at parking area.

19 Cycle the Coastal Trail

What: 11.75-mile road ride (Half Moon Bay). **Stage:** West Point parking lot, 22 West Point Ave., Moss Beach (37.503422°N / 122.494711°W). **Elevation differential:** 45 feet. **Route:** Out-and-back from the lot via Princeton Avenue, Broadway, Prospect Way, Capistrano Road, Pillar Point Harbor Road, Half Moon Bay Coastal Trail (paved path), Magellan Avenue, Mirada Road, Half Moon Bay Coastal Trail (paved path) to bridge just south of Poplar Beach (dirt path south of here); turn around and return via reverse of outbound route. Ride passes Princeton Harbor and several beaches, including (north-to-south) Mirada Surf, Naples, Roosevelt, Half Moon Bay (State Beach), Dunes, Elmar, Francis, and Poplar. Mavericks Beach is just west of the staging point.

20 Eden Landing Interpretation

What: 4.5-mile mountain bike ride (Union City). **Stage:** Eden Landing Ecological Reserve, end of Eden Landing Road, Union City (37.622044°N / 122.1225528°W). **Elevation differential:** 8 feet. **Route:** Lollipop with counter-clockwise loop interrupted by short out-and-back segment. Route is entirely out-and-back during duck hunting season (October to February) because of trail closures. From parking area, head south on entry road; bear left then right to cross bridge. Begin counterclockwise loop (Eden Landing Trail). Leave trail to the right for out-and-back on unnamed spur trail. Return to Eden Landing Trail. Continue past Archimedes Screw exhibit onto Seasonal Loop Trail (turn around here during duck hunting season). Both routes return to bridge to close the loop; return to parking lot via entry road.

21 Joaquin Miller Time

What: 3.1-mile mountain bike ride (Oakland). **Stage:** Sequoia Horse Arena, Joaquin Miller Park, 10013 Skyline Blvd. (park along roadside), Oakland (37.816047°N / 122.181536°W). **Elevation differential:** 155 feet. **Route:**

Clockwise loop from Sequoia Arena entry road (south, then east, parallel to Skyline Boulevard), merge with Big Trees Trail (paved), bear right at end of pavement to remain on Big Trees (now on dirt; rocky toward end), right on Sequoia Bayview Trail (some rocky segments; bear right at Chaparral Trail junction), leave Bayview Trail adjacent to Sequoia Arena, return to entry road, then north to Skyline Blvd.

22 Lafayette Reservoir Roleur

What: 2.75 mile road ride (Lafayette). **Stage:** Lafayette Reservoir, 3849 Mount Diablo Blvd., Lafayette (37.885261°N / 122.139931°W). **Elevation differential:** 58 feet. **Route:** Clockwise loop via paved perimeter path of Lafayette Reservoir (Shore Trail). Shared path; ride at a reduced speed.

23 Pickleweed Inlet Open Loop

What: 14.05-mile road ride (Marin County). **Stage:** Dunphy Park, Bridgeway and Napa Streets, Sausalito (37.861050°N / 122.488631°W). **Elevation differential:** 145 feet. **Route:** Lollipop with long out-and-back segment and short loop. From Dunphy Park, head north from Napa Street on path to Marinship Way, Harbor Drive, Mill Valley-Sausalito Bike Path (Bay Trail), right turn at bike traffic circle, head east over bridge on path, through Hauke Park, right on Hamilton Drive, right on US 101 frontage road (freeway west side), straight onto US 101 frontage road (freeway east side), Seminary Drive (right at Ricardo Road to remain on Seminary and begin loop), left on Strawberry Drive, left on Ricardo Lane (400-foot climb: 11.1% grade) to Seminary (close loop), and return via Seminary, US 101 frontage roads, Hamilton Drive, bike path through Hauke Park and over bridge, Mill Valley–Sausalito Bike Path (Bay Trail), Harbor Drive, Marinship Way, and path to Dunphy Park. (Note: short dirt segment on path near park.)

24 Sobrante Sojourn

What: 3.7-mile mountain bike ride (Richmond). **Stage:** Sobrante Ridge Regional Preserve, Coach Drive, Richmond (37.969933°N / 122.259244°W). **Elevation differential:** 496 feet. **Route:** Lollipop with a counterclockwise loop, from Coach Drive entry via Sobrante Ridge Trail (turn left after 200 feet; Bay Area Ridge Trail or BART), Morningside Trail (stay left at fork; steep downhill), Morningside Drive, left on walkway adjacent to May Community Center and Park (stairs toward the top), Mighty Mite Lane (left), Heavenly Ridge Lane (left), reenter preserve via Heavenly Ridge Trail, Manzanita Trail (left), right on Sobrante Ridge Trail (BART) to Coach Drive entry.

25 Spokin' Shades of San Leandro

What: 13.85-mile road ride (San Leandro). **Stage:** Oyster Bay Regional Shoreline, San Leandro (37.709450°N / 122.192314°W). **Elevation differential:** 33 feet. **Route:** Clockwise loop via bike path through Oyster Bay Regional Shoreline (Bay Trail), then west via path to Airport Drive path, Doolittle Drive (road), Farallon Drive (left), Wicks Boulevard, Lewelling Boulevard (left), Washington Avenue, Grant Avenue, right on bike path (Bay Trail) to Monarch Bay Drive, left (use caution) to Neptune Drive to Oyster Bay.

Want more? The following in Best Bike Rides San Francisco *are classified as easy: Angel Island Expedition (mountain), Burleigh-Murray Safari (mountain), Hayward Shoreline Dig (mountain), John Brooks Memorial Adventure (mountain), Point Pinole Mission (mountain), Redwood Shores Jaunt (road), and Round San Leandro Bay (road).*

References

Accardi, Catherine, *San Francisco Landmarks*, Arcadia Publishing, Charleston, SC, 2012.

"American Society of Civil Engineers Seven Wonders," www.asce.org (archived article from Jul. 19, 2010).

Andes, Roy H., "Open Range Law in the American West," in *Law in the Western United States*, Vol. 3, Gordon Morris Bakken, editor, University of Oklahoma Press, Norman, OK, 2000.

Ballantine, Richard, *Richard's 21st Century Bicycle Book*, Overlook Press, New York, NY, 2001.

Bateson, John, "The Suicide Magnet that is the Golden Gate Bridge," *Los Angeles Times*, Sep. 29, 2013.

California Department of Transportation (Caltrans), *2018 Traffic Volumes on the California State Highway System*, Division of Traffic Operations, California State Transportation Agency, State of California, Sacramento, 2019.

Cassady, Stephen, *Spanning the Gate*, Squarebooks, Oxford, MS, 1987 (commemorative edition).

Chappell, Gordon, "Historic California Posts: Fort Cronkhite," California State Military Museum, www.california militaryhistory.org, Dec. 22, 2015.

Crespi, Juan & Alan K. Brown, *A Description of Distant Roads: Original Journals of the First Expedition into California, 1769-1770*, San Diego State University Press, San Diego, CA, 2001.

Dreyfus, Philip J., *Our Better Nature: Environment & the Making of San Francisco*, University of Oklahoma Press, Norman, OK, 2008.

Environmental Protection Agency, "Basic Information About Landfills," www.epa.gov/landfills/. Retrieved Feb. 2020.

Fairley, Lincoln, *Mount Tamalpais: A History*, Scottwall Associates, San Francisco, CA, 1987.

Federal Aviation Administration, "Calendar Year 2019, Final, Revenue Enplanements at All Airports," Sep. 25, 2020, www.faa.gov/airports/planning_capacity/passenger_all cargo_stats/passenger/. Retrieved Oct. 2020.

Friend, Tad, "Jumpers: The Fatal Grandeur of the Golden Gate Bridge," *The New Yorker*, Vol. 79, No. 30, p. 48, Oct. 13, 2003.

Haller, Stephen & John A. Martini, *Last Missile Site: An Operational & Physical History of Nike Site SF-88, Fort Barry, California*, Hole in the Head Press, Bodega Bay, CA 2008.

Hansen, Gladys, *San Francisco Almanac*, 3rd edition, Chronicle Publishing, San Francisco, 1995.

Hice, Eric & Daniel Schierling, *Historical Study of Yerba Buena Island, Treasure Island, & their Buildings*, Mare Island Naval Shipyard, Vallejo, CA, 1996.

Hills of San Francisco, (compilation of San Francisco Chronicle articles), Chronicle Publishing, San Francisco, 1959.

Hogg, P.S., *Robert Burns–The Patriot Bard*, Mainstream Publishing, Edinburgh, Scotland, UK, 2008.

Jackson, Donald C., *Great American Bridges & Dams*, John Wiley & Sons, New York, NY, 1995.

Katz, Erica, *San Francisco's Golden Gate Park: A Thousand and Seventeen Acres of Stories*, Westwinds Press, Portland, OR, 2001.

Lightfoot, Kent & Otis Parrish, *California Indians & Their Environment: An Introduction*, University of California Press, Berkeley, CA, 2009.

McClintock, Elizabeth, T*he Trees of Golden Gate Park & San Francisco*, Publishers Press, Salt Lake City, UT, 2001.

NIchols, Nancy Ann, James Delahunty & Alan Hammond Nichols, *San Quentin: Inside the Walls*, San Quentin Museum Press, San Quentin, CA, 1991.

Nuttall, Donald A., "Gaspar de Portolá: Disenchanted Conquistador of Spanish Upper California," *Southern California Quarterly*, Vol. 53, No. 3, pp. 185-198, 1971.

Owens, T.O., *The Golden Gate Bridge*, Rosen Publishing Group, New York, NY, 2001.

Prado, Mark, "Did Marin Lose Out on BART?," *Marin Independent Journal*, Aug. 7, 2010.

Sierra Point Biotech Project Environmental Impact Report, State Clearinghouse #2006012024, City of Brisbane, CA. Prepared by LSA Associates, Inc., Berkeley, CA, Nov. 2006.

Starr, Kevin, *Golden Gate: The Life & Times of America's Greatest Bridge*, Bloomsbury Press, New York, NY, 2010.

"Trail Map of UCSF Mount Sutro Open Space Reserve," Mount Sutro Stewards & the University of California, San Francisco, www.peasepress.com/sutromap.pdf. Retrieved Oct. 2019.

Ungaretti, Lorri, *San Francisco's Sunset District*, Arcadia Publishing, Charleston, SC, 2003.

Weitz, Keith, Morton Barlaz, Ranji Ranjithan, Downey Brill, Susan Thorneloe, & Robert Ham, "Life Cycle Management of Municipal Solid Waste," in *The International Journal of Life Cycle Assessment*, Vol. 4, No. 4, July 1999, pp. 195-201.

Individual Bay Area city websites (please see "Resources" for list).

Alameda-Contra Costa (AC) Transit, www.actransit.org. Retrieved Jan.–Feb. 2020.

Bay Area Rapid Transit, www.bart.gov. Retrieved Feb. 2020.

Bay Area Ridge Trail, http://ridgetrail.org. Retrieved Feb. 2020.

Caltrain (California commuter rail), www.caltrain.com. Retrieved Feb. 2020.

County Connection, http://countyconnection.com. Retrieved Feb. 2020.

East Bay Municipal Utilities District, www.ebmud.org. Retrieved Dec. 2019.

East Bay Regional Parks District, www.ebparks.org. Retrieved over several months, 2019–2020.

Friends of Joaquin Miller Park, www.fojmp.org. Retrieved Jan.–Feb. 2020.

Golden Gate Bridge, www.goldengate.org/bridge/visiting-the-bridge/bikes-pedestrians/. Retrieved Dec. 2019.

Golden Gate National Recreation Area, www.nps.gov/goga. Retrieved over several months, 2019–2020.

Golden Gate Transit, www.goldengate.org/bus/. Retrieved Feb. 2020.

M.H. de Young Museum, https://deyoung.famsf.org/deyoung/. Retrieved Feb. 2020.

Marin County Parks, www.marincountyparks.org. Retrieved over several months, 2019–2020.

Marin Municipal Water District, www.marinwater.org. Retrieved Jan.–Feb. 2020.

Marin Transit, http://marintransit.org. Retrieved Feb. 2020.
National Register of Historic Places, www.nationalregisterofhistoricplaces.com. Retrieved Jan.–Feb. 2020.

San Francisco Bay Trail, http://baytrail.org. Retrieved over several months, 2019–2020.

San Francisco Municipal Transportation Agency (SFMTA), www.sfmta.org. Retrieved Feb. 2020.

San Francisco Neighborhood Map, www.jenniferrosdail.com. Retrieved Feb. 2020.

San Francisco Recreation & Parks, www.sfrecpark.org. Retrieved Nov. 2019.

San Francisco Urban Riders, http://sfurbanriders.org. Retrieved Feb. 2020.

Visit Half Moon Bay, www.visithalfmoonbay.org. Retrieved Feb. 2020.

Wikipedia articles (http://en.wikipedia.org) on Adolph Sutro, Alameda, Bolinas, Bolinas Lagoon, Fort Barry, Fort Cronkhite, Gaspar de Portolá, George Carroll (judge), Golden Gate Bridge, Golden Gate Park, list of California urban areas, list of islands of California, list of Longest Suspension Bridge Spans, Makoto Hagiwara, Marin County, Mount Sutro, Mount Tamalpais, Mountain biking, Novato, Open range, Point Richmond, Robert W. Crown, Rodeo Beach, Rodeo Lagoon, San Francisco, San Francisco Bay, San Francisco Bay Area, San Francisco-Oakland Bay Bridge, San Leandro, San Quentin State Prison, Sigmund Stern Recreation Grove, Sunset District, Sutro Tower, Treasure Island SF, University of California San Francisco, Yerba Buena Island.

About the Author

Wayne D. Cottrell is an engineering, math, and science educator specializing in transportation. He's also a researcher, author, runner, cyclist, snowshoer, and orienteerer. He is a member of the Transportation Research Board's Bicycles Committee and has been an active cyclist and member of USA Cycling for twenty-five years. His bicycle racing résumé includes occasional road and mountain bike wins. He won an award for his writing from the National Research Council in 1999. Wayne grew up in the Bay Area, in Oakland. He bicycled to college, then occasionally to work after graduating, and then for recreation and competition, becoming familiar with biking routes throughout California. Wayne is the author of *Road Biking Utah* and Best Bike Rides guide books for Los Angeles, Orange County, and San Francisco, all FalconGuides; seventeen articles on transportation in refereed technical journals; thirty technical articles in conference proceedings; and a number of transportation research reports. He earned a PhD in transportation engineering from the University of Utah in 1997 and is a registered traffic engineer in California. Wayne is a licensed Category 3 and Masters cyclist with USA Cycling. He currently resides in Searles Valley, California.